California DMV Exam

Workbook

Your Roadmap to Success | 500 Driving Questions and Answers in 8 Practice Tests Included

Jack Chaseley

Table of Contents

Chapter 1: Introduction

Why passing the California DMV exam is important

As a driving education specialist, I am delighted to give you with a detailed explanation of why passing the California DMV exam is so crucial. Passing the DMV test is the first step toward obtaining a driver's license, which is an important milestone for many people. But, apart from being a rite of passage, passing this exam is critical for various reasons.

To begin with, passing the California DMV exam is a legal requirement for driving a car in the state. If you are found driving on public roads without a valid driver's license, you may face legal repercussions. This might involve penalties, points on your driving record, and possibly license suspension or revocation. Driving without a license can also result in increased insurance costs, which can be a substantial financial hardship.

Passing the DMV exam also shows that you have the appropriate knowledge and abilities to drive safely on California highways. The test includes everything from basic traffic laws and regulations to sophisticated driving methods. By passing this exam, you demonstrate that you understand traffic laws and are prepared to drive in a variety of contexts, including highways and residential neighborhoods.

Passing the California DMV test can also lead to more mobility and freedom. Having a driver's license allows you to drive yourself to and from job, school, and other activities rather than relying on public transit or others. This is especially significant for people who reside in places with few public transit alternatives or who have mobility issues.

Passing the DMV test may also provide you with new work options. Many organizations demand a valid driver's license for specific occupations that entail travel, such as delivery drivers or sales reps. Passing the test shows potential employers that you have the relevant abilities and qualifications for these occupations.

Overview of the guide

In this section, I'll give you a rundown of what you can anticipate from the "California DMV Exam Workbook," a thorough resource designed to help you prepare for the California DMV written test. The book is designed to give you with the knowledge and abilities you need to pass the test on your first try.

The first portion of the book goes through the fundamentals of the California DMV exam, such as what to anticipate on test day, how to prepare for the exam, and what to do if you fail. This section also contains advice on how to manage your time throughout the test and how to tackle various sorts of questions.

The following portion of the book goes through the laws of the road, which is one of the most important aspects of the exam. This section contains information about California traffic rules and regulations, such as speed limits, traffic signals, and traffic signs. It also includes safe driving tactics, such as defensive driving strategies and how to deal with all sorts of weather and road conditions.

The third portion of the guide goes through the many sorts of driving scenarios that you can experience on the exam, such as highway driving, residential driving, and parking. This section contains advice on how to negotiate certain events safely and successfully, as well as frequent blunders to avoid.

To help you prepare for the exam, the fourth portion of the guide provides 500 sample questions grouped into eight practice exams. These questions cover all of the subjects covered in the previous parts and are intended to be as close to the actual test as possible. Answering these questions will help you discover areas that require more study as well as boost your confidence and familiarity with the exam style.

The book concludes with a bonus section that contains extra resources to help you prepare for the exam. This section contains a dictionary of significant driving words, a list of often used driving acronyms, and a list of relevant links and resources.

Throughout the guide, you will find clear, short explanations of key ideas, as well as helpful test hints and tactics. The book is intended to be simple to follow and comprehend, with the goal of giving you with the knowledge and abilities needed to pass the California DMV exam on your first attempt.

Test-taking strategies

There are various test-taking tactics you may employ to boost your chances of passing the California DMV exam, in addition to having a thorough awareness of the rules of the road and driving scenarios. In this area, I'll provide you some professional advice and recommendations on how to prepare for the test and enhance your success.

1. Carefully read the questions: Misreading the questions is one of the most typical errors that test participants make. Take your time and thoroughly study each question to ensure you understand what it is asking. Pay close attention to terms and phrases that might assist you in determining the correct response.

2. remove answers: If you're unsure of an answer, try to remove the options you know are erroneous. This increases your chances of selecting the correct answer. Remember that there is only one correct answer to each question, and that incorrect responses are intended to be plausible but ultimately erroneous.

3. Manage your time: Because the California DMV test is timed, efficient time management is essential. Try to keep a steady pace so that you have enough time to answer all of the questions. If you become stuck on a question, go on and return to it later if you have time.

4. Make advantage of your scratch paper: The DMV test includes scratch paper, which you may use to scribble down notes or do computations. Use this page to work through difficulties and arrange your thoughts, particularly for topics requiring math.

5. Take pauses: Because the DMV exam is long and demanding, it is critical to take breaks to rest your thoughts and refuel. Stretch, take deep breaths, and clear your thoughts throughout your pauses. However, don't spend too much time on breaks because you want to make the most of your time.

6. Practice, practice, practice: Practicing is one of the greatest strategies to prepare for the California DMV exam. Use the practice questions in this guide to assess your knowledge and find areas that require more research. The more you practice, the more at ease you'll feel with the exam structure and the more confident you'll feel on test day.

7. Maintain calm and attention: Finally, it is critical to maintain calm and focus during the exam. Maintain a calm demeanor and avoid being overly agitated or nervous. Take deep breaths, keep positive, and have faith in your planning. Remember that if you don't pass the first time, you may always repeat the test.

Chapter 2: California DMV Exam Overview

Exam format and structure

As a driving education specialist, I am pleased to present you with an explanation of the format and organization of the California DMV exam. Understanding the format of the exam is critical for efficient preparation and may help you approach the exam with confidence.

The DMV test in California is a written exam with 46 multiple-choice questions. The test is organized into three portions, each covering a distinct subject. These topics include traffic regulations, signs, and signals, safe driving techniques, and road rules.

The exam's first portion covers traffic regulations, signs, and signals. This section contains questions on California traffic rules and regulations such speed limits, right-of-way, and traffic signals and signs. It also includes information on school zones, train crossings, and pedestrian safety.

The second component of the exam focuses on safe driving techniques. This section contains questions about defensive driving practices include scanning the road, anticipating dangers, and keeping a safe following distance. It also discusses themes including driving while intoxicated, distracted driving, and the consequences of weariness on driving.

The third portion of the exam covers traffic laws. This section contains questions on various driving situations, such as merging onto a highway, handling intersections, and passing other vehicles. It also goes through issues like parking, turning, and backing up.

Each segment of the test has 15-16 questions, and you must answer at least 38 of them correctly to pass. You have 60 minutes to finish the exam, which is timed. Because the questions are chosen at random from a pool of prospective questions, each exam is unique.

The DMV test in California is given on a computer, and you will be given headphones to listen to the questions. You may also explore the exam and pick your answers using a keyboard and mouse. You can request accommodations, such as a magnifying glass or a sign language interpreter, if you have trouble reading or hearing the questions.

In short, the California DMV test is a written exam with 46 multiple-choice questions organized into three topics: traffic laws, signs, and signals; safe driving practices; and road regulations. Each segment of the test has 15-16 questions, and you must properly answer at least 38 of them to pass. The test is timed and given on a computer. Understanding the format and structure of the test is critical for efficient preparation and may help you approach the exam confidently.

Topics covered on the exam

In this part, I'll give you a rundown of the subjects included on the California DMV exam. The test covers a wide range of driving issues, including traffic rules and safe driving practices.

Traffic Laws, Signs, and Signals: Traffic laws, signs, and signals are one of the key subjects covered on the California DMV test. This section discusses fundamental road rules such as speed limits, right-of-way, and traffic lights. It also includes more particular restrictions, such as those governing school zones, railroad crossings, and pedestrian safety.

Safe Driving Techniques: Another important topic addressed in the exam is safe driving techniques. This section contains questions about defensive driving practices include scanning the road, anticipating dangers, and keeping a safe following distance. It also discusses themes including driving while intoxicated, distracted driving, and the consequences of weariness on driving.

Rules of the Road: The rules of the road are the final topic covered on the California DMV test. This section contains questions on various driving situations, such as merging onto a highway, handling intersections, and passing other vehicles. It also goes through issues like parking, turning, and backing up.

Other subjects that might be addressed on the test are:

- Vehicle safety and maintenance: This section addresses fundamental vehicle maintenance issues such as checking tire pressure and replacing a tire. It also discusses seat belt legislation and kid safety seats.

- Sharing the road: This section addresses how to share the road safely with other vehicles, pedestrians, and bikers. It covers subjects including overtaking bicyclists, ceding to emergency cars, and avoiding animal accidents.

- Special driving situations: This section addresses issues about driving in severe weather conditions, driving in construction zones, and driving on mountain routes.

- Driving obligations: This section addresses issues with driving responsibilities, such as reporting accidents and maintaining adequate insurance. It also discusses the hazards of driving while intoxicated and the penalties for breaking traffic regulations.

The questions on the California DMV exam are chosen at random from a pool of prospective questions, so each exam is unique. However, by studying the test subjects and preparing with sample questions, you can improve your chances of passing the exam on the first try.

Tips for studying effectively

Preparing for the California DMV exam necessitates efficient study approaches in order to pass the exam on the first try. In this part, I'll provide you professional guidance and recommendations on how to study efficiently for the test.

1. Make a study schedule: Creating a study timetable that works for you is the first step toward productive studying. Set aside time for studying each day or week, and stick to it. This will help you remain on track and cover all of the important subjects before the exam.

2. Utilize study resources: The California DMV offers study materials such as the California Driver Handbook and the DMV Exam Practice Test. Use these tools to review the test subjects and practice with example questions. Additional study resources can also be found online or in the form of study guides.

3. Take practice exams: Practice tests are a great method to measure your knowledge and find areas that require more study. Take practice exams on a regular basis and utilize the results to target your studies on the areas where you need to improve.

4. Study in a calm, distraction-free area: It's critical to study in a peaceful, distraction-free place where you can focus. Turn off your phone and other electrical gadgets, and try not to be interrupted by other people or dogs.

5. Use active learning tactics: Active learning approaches, such as taking notes, making flashcards, and summarizing knowledge, can help you recall information more effectively than passive learning techniques, such as reading or listening. Experiment with several active learning approaches to see what works best for you.

6. Study consistently: When it comes to good studying, consistency is essential. Don't pack all of your learning into a single session or day. Instead, study regularly over a longer period of time. This will improve your memory and minimize your tension and anxiety.

7. Take breaks: Breaks are necessary for good learning. Take brief pauses every hour or so to rest and replenish your batteries. Use the breaks to stretch, go for a stroll, or do something relaxing.

8. Get adequate sleep: Adequate sleep is necessary for good learning. Make an effort to obtain at least 7-8 hours of sleep every night, and avoid studying late at night. Sleep deprivation can decrease cognitive performance and make it difficult to remember knowledge.

9. Maintain organization: Keep your study materials organized and in one location. Keep track of your notes, practice exams, and other study materials using folders, binders, or online resources. This will allow you to stay focused and save time hunting for materials.

To summarize, effective studying techniques for the California DMV exam include creating a study schedule, using study materials, taking practice tests, studying in a quiet environment, using active studying techniques, studying consistently, taking breaks, getting enough sleep, and staying organized. You may improve your chances of passing the California DMV test on your first try by following these professional ideas and recommendations.

Chapter 3: Traffic Laws and Road Signs

Understanding traffic laws and regulations in California

Understanding California's traffic rules and regulations is critical for safe and responsible driving. As a driving education specialist, I am delighted to offer you with an overview of California's traffic rules and regulations.

Speed Limits:

California speed restrictions vary based on the kind of road, location, and time of day. Most California roads have a speed restriction of 65 miles per hour, but most rural two-lane highways have a speed limit of 55 miles per hour. The speed restriction in residential areas and around schools is frequently 25 miles per hour or less.

Right-of-Way:

The legal right of a car or pedestrian to move first in a given scenario is referred to as right-of-way. Drivers in California must surrender the right of way to pedestrians crossing the roadway in a designated or unmarked crosswalk. Drivers must also give way to emergency vehicles, school buses, and other vehicles with the right of way.

Signs and Traffic Signals:

Traffic signals and signs are used to control traffic and keep cars and pedestrians safe. Drivers in California must observe traffic signals and signs, such as stop signs, yield signs, and traffic lights. Ignoring or removing traffic cones, barriers, or other traffic control equipment is likewise prohibited.

Seat Belt and Child Safety Seat Requirements:

Seat belts are required to be worn by all drivers and passengers in California. Children under the age of eight must be fastened in an appropriate car seat or booster seat for their age, weight, and height. Rear-facing car seats are required for children under the age of two.

Distracted Driving Regulations:

Distracted driving is a major cause of accidents on California highways. Drivers in California are not permitted to use portable electronic devices while driving, including mobile phones, iPads, and GPS systems. Texting and driving is also prohibited in California.

Driving While Intoxicated Laws:

Driving while high on drugs or alcohol is banned in California. California has a zero-tolerance policy for drivers under the age of 21 who are under the influence of alcohol or drugs. The legal blood alcohol content (BAC) level for drivers over the age of 21 is 0.08%.

Passing and Changing Lanes Regulations:

Drivers in California must pass on the left and may only do so when it is safe to do so. Before changing lanes, drivers must signal their desire and establish that it is safe to do so.

Common road signs and their meanings

Road signs are an important aspect of traffic management since they help to guarantee the safety of all vehicles and pedestrians on the road. As a driving education specialist, I am glad to present you with an overview of frequent traffic signs and their explanations.

Stop Signs:

Stop signs, which are red octagonal signs with white writing, signal that automobiles must come to a complete stop before continuing. Drivers must come to a complete stop behind the stop line or crosswalk and cede the right-of-way to other vehicles and pedestrians.

Yield Signs:

Yield signs are red and white triangle signs that warn drivers to slow down and give way to other cars and pedestrians. If required, drivers must come to a complete stop and wait for the road to clear before proceeding.

Speed Limit Signs:

Speed limit signs show the fastest speed that cars are permitted to go on a certain route or highway. Typically, speed limit signs are rectangular with black letters on a white backdrop. Speed limit signs may be yellow or orange in some circumstances.

Lane Control Signs:

Lane control signs indicate which lanes are open and which are blocked to traffic. Typically, lane control signs are rectangular with black characters on a white backdrop or white letters on a black background.

Warning Signs:

Warning signs are yellow and diamond-shaped, and they identify possible traffic hazards. Sharp bends, steep slopes, and tiny bridges are examples of potential risks. Warning signs are intended to inform drivers to potentially hazardous circumstances and encourage them to drive cautiously.

Regulatory Signs:

Regulatory signs are white and rectangular in shape, and they display traffic laws or regulations. Speed limit signs, stop signs, yield signs, and no parking signs are examples of these signs.

Construction Signs:

Orange construction signs indicate construction zones or roadwork ahead. Lane closures, diversions, and lower speed restrictions are examples of these signs.

Construction signs are intended to warn drivers of changes in traffic patterns and to encourage them to drive cautiously.

School Zone Signs:

School zone signs are normally yellow and warn vehicles to slow down and be cautious in places where children may be present. Speed limit decreases, crossing guards, and flashing lights are examples of these indicators.

No Parking Signs:

No parking signs denote places where parking is not permitted. These signs can be seen in places where parking is prohibited, such as fire lanes, loading zones, and limited access areas.

Safe driving practices

Driving safely is critical for avoiding accidents and guaranteeing the safety of all drivers and pedestrians on the road. As a driving education specialist, I am pleased to offer you with an overview of safe driving behaviors that you should employ on California roadways.

1. Wear Your Seat Belt: One of the most important things you can do to keep safe on the road is to wear your seat belt. In the case of an accident, seat belts can save lives and avoid major injuries.

2. Obey Speed restrictions: Speed restrictions are in place to guarantee the safety of all road users, including pedestrians. Follow established speed restrictions and alter your speed to account for road conditions like rain or snow.

3. Avoid Distracted Driving: Distracted driving is a major cause of accidents on California highways. While driving, avoid using your phone, eating, or indulging in other activities. Maintain a constant concentration on the road.

4. Maintain a Safe gap: Maintain a safe gap between your car and the vehicle ahead of you. This allows you to respond rapidly to traffic changes and helps to avoid accidents.

5. Use Turn Signals: Using turn signals allows other drivers to anticipate your actions, which helps to avoid accidents. When changing lanes, turning, or merging onto a motorway, use your turn signals.

6. Obey Right-of-Way laws: Obey right-of-way laws and yield to other drivers as needed. Yielding to pedestrians in crosswalks, emergency vehicles, and other drivers when merging onto a motorway are all examples of this.

7. Avoid Driving Under the Influence: Driving under the influence of drugs or alcohol is unlawful in California and puts your life and the lives of others at danger. If you intend to consume alcohol, appoint a sober driver or use public transit.

Stay awake: While driving, stay awake and aware of your surroundings. Keep an eye out for possible risks including pedestrians, bikers, and other cars.

9. Maintain Your car: Keep your car in good functioning order by doing regular maintenance. This involves completing regular oil changes and tune-ups, as well as inspecting your brakes, tires, and lights.

10. Be Patient: Be patient and respectful to other road users. Avoid aggressive driving habits like tailgating or cutting other cars off.

Chapter 4: Driver's Responsibility

Responsibilities of drivers in California

As a California driver, you have specific duties to guarantee your own and other people's safety on the road. As a driving education specialist, I am pleased to offer you with an overview of California drivers' obligations.

1. Obtaining a Driver's License: You must obtain a driver's license before you may legally drive in California. Passing a written test, a driving test, and giving confirmation of identification and residence are all required.

2. Obeying Traffic Laws and Regulations: California drivers are required to abide by all traffic laws and regulations, including speed limits, right-of-way restrictions, and traffic signals and signs. Ignoring or removing traffic control devices is also prohibited.

3. Driving Safely: California drivers must always drive safely and responsibly. This includes adhering to speed restrictions, avoiding distractions, and keeping a safe gap between cars.

4. Vehicle Maintenance: Drivers in California are responsible for keeping their vehicles in excellent functioning order. This involves routine maintenance like as oil changes and tire rotations, as well as checking that all lights and brakes work properly.

5. Having Adequate Insurance: Drivers in California are obliged to have adequate insurance coverage for their vehicle. This includes liability insurance to cover any damages or injuries you cause to other people while driving.

6. Accident Reporting: If you are involved in an accident in California, you must report it to the police or highway patrol if the injury, death, or property damage exceeds $1,000.

7. Yielding to Emergency Vehicles: In California, drivers must yield to emergency vehicles with lights and sirens, such as police cars, fire engines, and ambulances.

Drivers in California are obliged to carry valid identification, such as a driver's license or a state-issued identity card, at all times when driving.

9. Medical Conditions: If you have a medical condition that may impair your ability to drive safely, you must notify the California Department of Motor Vehicles (DMV).

10. Cooperation with Law Enforcement: In California, drivers are obligated to comply with law enforcement agents when they are approached. This involves presenting identity, proof of insurance, and submitting to sobriety tests if suspected of driving while intoxicated.

Sharing the road with other drivers, pedestrians, and cyclists

It is critical for drivers in California to share the road with other vehicles, pedestrians, and bicycles. Sharing the road in a safe and responsible manner is an important component of being a responsible driver and guaranteeing the safety of all road users. As a driving education specialist, I am pleased to present you with an overview on how to share the road with other cars, pedestrians, and bicycles.

Road Sharing with Other Drivers:

It is critical to respect traffic laws and regulations when sharing the road with other cars, such as speed limits, right-of-way restrictions, and traffic lights and signs. Maintaining a safe distance between cars and avoiding distracted driving are also key. Use your turn signals to warn other drivers of your intentions if you need to change lanes or join onto a motorway.

Road Sharing with Pedestrians:

It is critical to yield to pedestrians in crosswalks and at crossings while sharing the road with them. It's also a good idea to keep an eye out for pedestrians who are strolling on the sidewalk or crossing the roadway outside of a crosswalk. Always yield to people crossing the roadway when passing a stopped bus.

Road Sharing with Cyclists:

It is critical to allow bikers ample space and avoid passing too closely when sharing the road. Cyclists, like any other vehicle, have the right to use the road, and it is critical to respect their space. Always check your blind zones for cyclists who may be riding beside or behind you when turning or merging.

Tips for Safe Road Sharing:

1. Be Patient: Show patience and courtesy to other drivers. Avoid aggressive driving habits including tailgating and cutting off other automobiles or bikes.

2. Use Your Signals: Use your turn signals to notify other drivers of your intentions. This involves merging, changing lanes, turning, and stopping.

3. Check Your Blind Spots: When changing lanes or merging, always check your blind spots to verify that there are no other road users in your path.

4. Avoid Distracted Driving: Avoid using your phone or indulging in other activities that may cause you to become distracted while driving. Maintain a constant concentration on the road.

5. Yield the Right-of-Way: When necessary, yield the right-of-way to other road users. Pedestrians in crosswalks and bikers on the road are included.

6. Maintain a safe distance between your vehicle and other road users, including bicycles and pedestrians. This enables you to respond fast and avoid mishaps.

7. Be Aware of Your Surroundings: Keep an eye out for possible risks like as pedestrians, cyclists, or other cars at all times.

Distracted driving and its consequences

Distracted driving is a major source of accidents on California highways, with catastrophic repercussions for drivers, passengers, and pedestrians. As a driving education specialist, I am pleased to offer you with an overview of distracted driving and its repercussions.

Any action that diverts a driver's attention away from the road is considered distracted driving. Using a telephone, texting, eating, drinking, applying cosmetics, changing the radio, or conversing with passengers are all examples. Distracted driving is defined as anything that takes your eyes off the road, your hands off the wheel, or your thoughts off driving.

Distracted Driving Consequences:

1. Accidents: Distracted driving is a major cause of car accidents on California highways. According to the California DMV, 3,540 persons were killed or wounded in distracted driving incidents in 2019.

2. Injuries and Deaths: Distracted driving can result in significant injuries and deaths. In 2019, 276 individuals were killed in distracted driving incidents in California.

3. Legal Implications: It is prohibited in California to use a smartphone while driving, unless you are using it hands-free. Infringing on this legislation might result in penalties and points on your license. You might face criminal prosecution if you cause an accident while using your telephone.

4. Increased Insurance premiums: If you get in an accident while distracted driving, your insurance premiums may skyrocket.

5. Emotional and Psychological Consequences: Being in a vehicle accident can be distressing, and the emotional and psychological effects can continue for a long time after the event.

Avoiding Distracted Driving:

1. Remove Your Phone: Remove your phone while driving, or use it hands-free if you need to make a call or send a text.

2. Plan Ahead: Before you start driving, plan your itinerary and make any required changes.

3. Do Not Eat or Drink While Driving: Do not eat or drink while driving. If you need to eat or drink something, pull over to a safe spot.

4. Secure Loose goods: Keep loose goods in your car secure to avoid them rolling around and disturbing you while driving.

5. Maintain Your Focus on the Road: Maintain your focus on the road and prevent any activity that may divert your attention away from driving.

6. Pull Over if Necessary: If you need to make a call, send a text, or do anything else that takes your undivided concentration, pull over to a safe spot.

Chapter 5: Vehicle Operation and Control

Vehicle safety and control

Driving in California places a premium on both the driver's and the passenger's sense of safety and control. Accidents can be avoided and the safety of all drivers and passengers on the road improved by keeping one's car in good repair and employing safe driving practices. I am glad to give you with an overview of vehicle safety and control as an authority in the field of driver education, and I look forward to doing so.

Security of Vehicles:

1. Routine Maintenance It is absolutely necessary to do routine maintenance on your vehicle in order to guarantee both its safety and its dependability. This involves doing brake inspections, changing the oil, and rotating the tires.

2. Check Your Lights You should do routine maintenance checks on your headlights, taillights, and turn signals to verify that they are in good working order. This is of utmost significance during the nighttime or in situations with limited visibility.

3. Inspect Your Tires You should check the pressure in your tires on a regular basis and verify that they have an appropriate amount of tread depth. This has the potential to enhance traction on the road and reduce the risk of blowouts.

4. examine Your Brakes It is important to examine your brakes on a regular basis and replace the brake pads as necessary. Brakes that are in good working order can help prevent accidents and ensure that you will be able to come to a halt swiftly in the case of an emergency.

5. Wear a Seat Belt At all times, you should wear a seat belt and you should make sure that everyone else in your car does the same. When worn, seat belts have the potential to prevent fatalities and serious injuries in the event of a collision.

Control of the Vehicle:

1. Maintain a Safe gap Between Your car and the Vehicle in Front of You Always maintain a safe gap between your car and the vehicle in front of you. This enables you to respond rapidly in the event that you are unexpectedly stopped or face any other kind of emergency.

2. Obey the Speed restrictions: Obey the speed restrictions that are posted and change your speed according to the circumstances of the road. When traveling in adverse weather or on roads you are not acquainted with, reduce your speed.

3. Make Use of Your Turn Signals When changing lanes or turning, make use of your turn signals to express your intentions to other drivers. This makes it easier for other drivers to predict your movements and prevent collisions with you.

4. Stay Focused on Driving Stay focused on the road at all times by avoiding activities that might divert your attention, such as texting, eating, or adjusting the radio. Always remember to keep your attention on the road in front of you.

5. Adjust Your Mirrors You should make sure that you have a good vision of your surroundings by adjusting both your side mirrors and your rearview mirror. This can assist in the prevention of accidents and increase the overall safety of your driving.

6. Make Sure to Use Your Brakes Instead of depending on downshifting or other ways, make sure to use your brakes when you need to slow down or stop your car. This guarantees that you will be able to come to a halt promptly in the event of an emergency.

Proper use of safety devices, such as seat belts and airbags

The correct use of safety equipment, such as seat belts and airbags, is a crucial component of driving a vehicle and maintaining control of it in the state of California. In the case of an accident, safety equipment can assist reduce the likelihood of injuries and perhaps save lives. I am delighted to offer you with an overview of the appropriate way to utilize safety gadgets in light of the fact that I am an expert in the field of driver education.

Seat Belts:

1. Always Wear Your Seat Belt: Always wear your seat belt when driving or riding in a vehicle. This pertains to the driver as well as any and all passengers.

2. Adjust Your Seat Belt You should adjust your seat belt such that it crosses your chest and hips in a manner that is comfortable and secure. Because of this, you can be confident that it will offer the highest level of protection possible in the case of an accident.

3. Always Wear Both the Lap and Shoulder Belts For the utmost level of safety, always wear both the lap and shoulder belts. Both the shoulder belt and the lap belt should be worn correctly. The lap belt should be worn low over the hips, and the shoulder belt should be worn across the chest and shoulder.

4. Make Sure Children Have Appropriate Safety Restraints Children of all ages and sizes need to have appropriate safety restraints in the form of car seats or booster seats, respectively. Always ensure that you are following the directions provided by the manufacturer.

Airbags:

1. Use Seat Belts with Airbags: Always use your seat belt in conjunction with your airbag. Seat belts and airbags are meant to function together to offer the highest level of safety possible in the case of an accident.

2. Move Your Seat Back You should move your seat back at least ten inches so that you are not directly in front of the steering wheel. When the airbag goes off, you will be kept at a comfortable distance from it thanks to this feature.

3. Keep Your Hands on the Steering Wheel In the event that the airbag goes off, it is important to keep both of your hands on the steering wheel in the 9 and 3 o'clock positions to protect yourself from any injuries.

4. Replace Deployed or Damaged Airbags As soon as possible, you should replace your airbag if it has been deployed or if it has been damaged. In the case of a collision, an airbag that has sustained damage may not deploy as intended or may increase the risk of harm.

Child Safety Seats:

1. Always Follow the Manufacturer's Instructions When Installing and Using a Child Safety Seat Always follow the instructions provided by the manufacturer when installing and using a child safety seat.

2. Always Transport Infants in a Rear-Facing Car Seat: When transporting infants, always position them in a car seat that faces the rear of the vehicle. In the case of a collision, this offers the highest possible level of protection.

3. Seats That Facing Forward for Toddlers Toddlers need to be secured in forward-facing car seats that have a harness and should be put in the rear seat of the vehicle.

4. Booster Seats for Older Children Older children should use booster seats until they are tall enough to utilize a seat belt correctly. Booster seats are designed to raise the child's seat up to the appropriate height. Always ensure that you are following the directions provided by the manufacturer.

In a nutshell, it is required for the operation and control of a vehicle to make appropriate use of safety equipment such as seat belts and airbags in the state of California. Always use your seat belt, make sure it's adjusted correctly, and make sure you use both the lap and shoulder belts for the utmost protection. Adjust your seat and retain both hands on the steering wheel while using your airbag in conjunction with your seat belt. Also, use your airbag. When installing and using kid safety seats, make sure to follow the directions provided by the manufacturer. Additionally, make sure to use a seat that is suitable for your child's age as well as their size. If you follow these guidelines, you can reduce the risk of injuries and improve the overall safety of everyone who is riding in your car.

Handling emergency situations

In the state of California, operating a vehicle and maintaining control of it includes the responsibility of responding appropriately to unforeseen circumstances. Knowing how to respond in a crisis may help prevent accidents and save lives. Emergencies can happen at any moment, and being prepared for them is important. I am delighted to give you with an overview of how to handle emergency circumstances in light of the fact that I am an expert in the field of driving instruction.

Failure of the Brakes:

1. Pump the Brakes In the event that your vehicle's brakes fail to function, you should swiftly pump the brakes in order to build up pressure in the brake lines. It's possible that this will assist your car slow down.

2. Apply the Emergency Brake In order to slow down your car, you should apply the emergency brake. If you want to prevent your car from skidding, you should draw the emergency brake lever gently and gradually rather than pulling it with force.

3. change down: If you want to slow your car down, you should change down to a lower gear. Your speed might be lowered as a result, which will assist you avoid a collision.

4. Blow Your Horn Use the horn on your vehicle to draw the attention of other cars to the problem. Because of this, it is possible to reduce the risk of other cars colliding with yours.

Find a Safe area to Stop Your car The fifth step is to find a safe area to stop your car, such as the shoulder of the road or a parking lot. Make sure you give the other drivers a clear indication of what you intend to do.

A Blowout in the Tire:

1. Maintain a solid grasp: When driving, it is important to maintain a solid grasp on the steering wheel and to not freak out. Your car may veer off course if one of its tires blows out, but it is essential that you keep control of it.

2. Ease Off the Gas Pedal You may slow down by easing off the gas pedal in a calm and steady manner. It is important to avoid applying the brakes too quickly, since this might cause your car to slide.

3. Maintain a Straight Course You should maintain a straight course and not attempt to turn or change lanes at any point. This might result in you losing control of your car.

4. Make Your Intentions Known to Other Drivers After making your intentions known to other motorists, seek for a safe area to pull over.

5. Change the Tire If you don't have a spare tire, you should change the flat tire with one of those, or you should ask for help.

Vehicle Fire:

1. Pull Over: If you see flames or smell smoke, you should immediately stop the vehicle and go to a safe location.

2. Turn off the Engine 2. Before leaving the car, be sure the engine is turned off. Do not open the hood since doing so may enable oxygen to be drawn into the fire and ignite it more.

3. Put Out the Fire With an Extinguisher If you have access to an extinguisher, you should put out the fire by using it. Instead of aiming the extinguisher at the flames, you should point it at the source of the fire.

4. Make a Call for Help Make a call for help to the local fire department or to a business that provides roadside assistance.

Accidents:

1. Conduct an Injury Check Perform an injury check on both yourself and any other passengers. In the event that someone sustains an injury, dial 911 immediately.

2. take Your Vehicle to a Safe Location If your vehicle can still be driven, you should take it to a secure location away from the roadway as soon as possible.

3. Exchange Information Speak to the other motorist and exchange information with them, including your names, your phone numbers, and your insurance information.

4. Take photographs: After the collision, you should take photographs of the situation, including the damage done to the cars and the space around them.

5. Contact Your Insurance Company You should contact your insurance company to report the accident and to begin the claims process.

In a nutshell, responding appropriately to unexpected events is a vital component of operating and controlling a vehicle in the state of California. In the event that your brakes fail, you should pump them, engage the emergency brake, shift into a lower gear, honk the horn, and search for a spot to stop where it is safe to do so. Maintain a firm hold on the steering wheel, ease off the gas pedal, maintain a straight course, communicate your intentions, and change the tire if you have a tire blowout. In the event that your car catches fire, pull over to the side of the road, shut off the engine, and then use a fire extinguisher before calling for help. In the case of a collision, it is imperative that you check for injuries, relocate your car to a secure location, exchange information with other parties involved, take photographs, and contact your insurance provider. You may make yourself a more responsible and secure driver on the highways of California by following the advice in this article.

Chapter 6: Driving Under the Influence

Effects of alcohol and drugs on driving ability

In California, there is a substantial worry over the impact of alcohol and drugs on a person's ability to drive, and these effects can have severe repercussions. Driving while under the influence of alcohol or drugs is a criminal offense that can lead to monetary fines, the suspension or revocation of a driver's license, and even possible jail time. I am pleased to present you with an overview of the impact that alcohol and drugs have on a person's ability to drive because I am an expert in the field of driver education.

Alcohol:

Alcohol is a depressant that affects the central nervous system and can impair driving ability in several ways:

1. Impaired Judgment Alcohol can impair judgment and decision-making abilities, making it difficult to assess risk and make safe driving decisions. This can make it more dangerous to drive when under the influence of alcohol.

2. Decreased Coordination Because alcohol has the potential to impair coordination, it will be more difficult to maintain control of the vehicle and carry out fundamental driving duties including accelerating, stopping, and turning.

3. Alcohol may delay response time, making it difficult to respond quickly to unexpected events such as a pedestrian crossing the road or a car abruptly stopping in front of you. This makes it more dangerous to drink and drive. 3. Reduced response Time Alcohol can slow reaction time, making it more dangerous for drivers to drink and drive.

4. Decreased Vision Consuming alcohol can reduce one's vision, making it more difficult to see properly and more difficult to gauge distances and speeds effectively.

5. Drowsiness Alcohol may promote drowsiness, which can lead to exhaustion as well as a lower level of awareness, all of which can affect a person's ability to drive.

Drugs:

It is possible for drugs to impair one's ability to drive in a number of different ways, depending on the substance and how an individual reacts to it.

1. Impaired Judgment Drugs have the potential to impair one's judgment as well as one's ability to make judgments, which makes it more difficult to evaluate risks and select safe driving options.

2. Decreased Coordination Because of the potential for drugs to impair coordination, it may become more challenging to maintain control of the vehicle and carry out routine driving responsibilities.

3. Decreased Ability to React swiftly: The use of drugs can delay one's response time, making it more difficult to respond swiftly to unforeseen events.

4. Drowsiness: Some medicines can produce drowsiness, which can lead to exhaustion as well as a lower level of awareness, all of which can affect a person's ability to drive.

5. Distorted Perception: Some drugs can produce distorted perception, which makes it difficult to correctly evaluate distances, speeds, and other critical information. This can make it dangerous to consume these substances.

6. Aggressive Behavior Certain medicines might create behavior that is aggressive or reckless, which can increase the chance of being involved in an accident or other potentially hazardous circumstance.

7. Hallucinations: Certain medicines have the potential to create hallucinations, which can result in confusion and disorientation, both of which can impair a person's ability to drive.

Use in Combination:

It is possible for alcohol and drugs to have a synergistic impact, which would mean that the combination would impair a person's ability to drive much more than the effects of either substance would on their own. This is highly hazardous and has the potential to result in life-threatening mishaps and injuries.

Legal Limits:

It is against the law to operate a motor vehicle in the state of California with a blood alcohol content (BAC) of 0.08% or higher. The legal limit for drivers under the age of 21 is 0.01% or higher of blood alcohol content. In addition, it is against the law to operate a motor vehicle while under the influence of any substance, whether it be a prescription medicine or an over-the-counter medication that might affect a person's ability to drive.

Penalties:

Depending on the severity of the incident as well as the driver's driving history, the penalties for driving under the influence in California can range from fines to the suspension or revocation of the driver's license to even jail time.

California DUI laws and penalties

The regulations and penalties pertaining to DUI in California are severe, and breaking them can have severe repercussions. Driving while under the influence of alcohol or drugs is a criminal offense that can lead to monetary fines, the suspension or revocation of a driver's license, and even possible jail time. I am delighted to offer you with an overview of the rules and penalties pertaining to DUI in the state of California since I am an expert in the field of driver education.

Legal Limits:

It is against the law to operate a motor vehicle in the state of California with a blood alcohol content (BAC) of 0.08% or higher. The legal limit for drivers under the age of 21 is 0.01% or higher of blood alcohol content. The legal limit for commercial drivers is 0.04% or higher of blood alcohol content. In addition, it is against the law to operate a motor vehicle while under the influence of any substance, whether it be a prescription medicine or an over-the-counter medication that might affect a person's ability to drive.

Penalties:

Depending on the severity of the incident as well as the driver's driving history, the penalties for driving under the influence in California can range from fines to the suspension or revocation of the driver's license to even jail time. In California, the following are some of the consequences that might result from a first-time DUI conviction:

1. The fines might run anywhere from $390 to $1,000, in addition to any other penalty assessments that may be imposed.

2. Suspension of Driver's License: The individual's permission to operate a motor vehicle will be revoked for a period of time that ranges from four to twelve months. After a predetermined amount of time has passed, the driver may in some instances become eligible for a restricted license.

3. Probation: The driver may be placed on probation for a period of up to three years, during which time they are required to comply with specific requirements, such as attending DUI school, refraining from using alcohol and drugs, and submitting to chemical testing. Probation can be extended if the driver successfully completes the terms of the probation.

4. Possible Imprisonment The motorist faces the possibility of serving a jail term ranging from a minimum of two days to a maximum of six months.

5. Ignition Interlock Device The driver may be forced to have an ignition interlock device (IID) installed on their car. This device stops the vehicle from starting if the driver is found to have alcohol on their breath when the device is activated.

The penalties for repeat crimes of driving under the influence of alcohol are increased. For instance, the following are some of the consequences that one faces if they are convicted of a second DUI violation within ten years of their first conviction:

1. The fines might run anywhere from $390 to $1,000, in addition to any other penalty assessments that may be imposed.

2. Suspension of Driver's License: The individual's permission to operate a motor vehicle will be revoked for a period of time that ranges from one to two years. After a predetermined amount of time has passed, the driver may in some instances become eligible for a restricted license.

3. Probation: The motorist may be placed on probation for a period of up to five years, during which time they are required to comply with specific requirements, such as attending DUI school, refraining from using alcohol and drugs, and

submitting to chemical testing. Probation can be extended if the driver successfully completes the terms of their sentence.

4. Possible Imprisonment The motorist faces the possibility of serving a jail term ranging from a minimum of 96 hours to a maximum of one year.

5. Ignition Interlock Device The driver may be forced to have an ignition interlock device (IID) installed on their car. This device stops the vehicle from starting if the driver is found to have alcohol on their breath when the device is activated.

6. Impoundment of the Driver's Vehicle: The driver's vehicle may be detained for a period of up to one month.

Contributing Factors:

In addition to the penalties that have been detailed above, there are a number of aggravating circumstances that can make the consequences for DUI in California even more severe. These factors are as follows:

1. If the driver's blood alcohol concentration (BAC) is 0.15% or higher or higher, the penalties may be increased.

2. Refusal to Submit to Chemical Testing The penalties may be increased if the motorist refuses to submit to chemical testing. This is the second most common reason for increased penalties.

3. Previous convictions for driving under the influence If the motorist in question has a history of driving under the influence, the penalties may be increased.

4. Injuries or Death: If the motorist causes an injury or death while driving under the influence, the consequences may be more severe. These penalties may include felony charges and considerable amounts of time spent in jail.

Defense Strategies:

Depending on the specifics of the case, a defendant charged with DUI has access to a variety of potential defense options. These various tactics are as follows:

1. If you want to challenge the stop, you have to demonstrate that it was unlawful and that it wasn't based on reasonable suspicion or probable cause.

2. Challenging the Results of the Field Sobriety Tests In order to successfully challenge the results of the field sobriety tests, they must have been accurately given and analyzed.

3. Contesting the findings of Chemical Tests The findings of the chemical tests ought to have been acquired in an appropriate and correct manner.

4. Dispute the Results of the Blood Alcohol Content Calculation The BAC calculation must have been carried out correctly and based on reasonable assumptions.

Tips for avoiding DUI charges

As a driving education specialist, I am delighted to provide you advice on avoiding DUI charges. Driving while intoxicated (DUI) is a serious violation with significant repercussions. Here are some pointers to help you avoid DUI charges and become a more responsible and safe driver on California highways.

1. Plan ahead of time:

If you intend to drink, make arrangements for a safe trip home. This may entail hiring a designated driver, employing a ride-sharing service, or taking public transportation. It's critical to establish these plans before you start drinking so you don't have to make a decision when you're inebriated.

2. Avoid Relying on the Legal Limit:

In California, the legal limit for blood alcohol concentration (BAC) is 0.08%, however this does not indicate that it is safe to drive at this level. Driving abilities may be reduced even at lower BAC levels, therefore it's better to avoid driving after drinking entirely.

3. Stay away from certain medications:

Some prescription and OTC drugs can impair your driving skills, so check the labels and see your doctor or pharmacist if you're unsure. If a medicine has the potential to impair your driving skills, you should avoid driving until the medication has worn off.

4. Recognize Your Limits:

Everyone has various alcohol intake limitations, so it's crucial to be aware of your own and drink sensibly. If you begin to feel drowsy, stop drinking and wait until you are sober before driving again.

5. Maintain Hydration:

Staying hydrated and reducing the effects of alcohol on your body can be accomplished by drinking water or non-alcoholic beverages. It is critical to drink enough of water before to, during, and after consuming alcohol.

6. Consume Food Before Drinking:

Eating a meal before drinking can assist to decrease the absorption of alcohol into your system, so minimizing the effects of alcohol on your body.

7. Under no circumstances should you drink and drive:

The most efficient approach to prevent a DUI ticket is to never, ever drink and drive. Even though you feel OK, you might be impaired and endangering yourself and others.

8. Keep an Eye on Your Friends:

If you're out with drinking pals, make sure they have a safe trip home. Offer to be the designated driver or assist them in finding a safe transport. Don't allow your buddies drive when intoxicated.

9. Be Prepared in Case of Emergencies:

In case you need assistance or a ride home, keep a list of emergency contacts in your car or on your phone. A friend or family member, a cab or ride-sharing service, or a roadside assistance program are all options.

10. Go to a DUI School:

If you have been convicted of a DUI, going to a DUI school can teach you about the hazards of drinking and driving and how to prevent it in the future. It may also assist you in meeting court requirements and reducing the penalty for your violation.

Chapter 7: Conclusion

Tips for managing test anxiety and staying focused on exam day

As a driving education specialist, I am delighted to provide you advice on how to manage test anxiety and stay focused on exam day. Taking the California DMV written exam might be difficult, but with the appropriate preparation and mentality, you can overcome test anxiety and do well. Here are some strategies for dealing with test anxiety and remaining focused on exam day.

1. Get Ready Ahead of Time:

Preparing ahead of time is one of the most effective techniques to decrease test anxiety. Make sure you understand the subject and have properly studied the California DMV driving manual. Take practice examinations to become acquainted with the format and scheduling of the exam.

2. Get a Restful Night's Sleep:

Sleep is essential for cognitive function and memory, so obtain a full night's rest before the exam. This will assist you in being aware and concentrated during the exam.

3. Consume a Healthy Meal:

Eating a nutritious lunch before the exam might help you focus and stay awake. Avoid meals that are heavy or oily since they might make you feel lethargic. Instead, eat a well-balanced meal with protein, complex carbs, and healthy fats.

4. Be on time:

Arriving at the testing facility early might help you feel more at ease and prepared. This will allow you to check in, use the toilet, and settle yourself before the test begins.

5. Make Use of Relaxation Techniques:

Use relaxation techniques such as deep breathing, visualization, or progressive muscle relaxation if you are apprehensive or agitated before the exam. These approaches can assist you in calming your thoughts and reducing worry.

6. Maintain Concentration During the Exam:

It is critical to keep attentive and avoid distractions throughout the exam. Don't be concerned with what other test takers are doing or how quickly they are completing the exam. Concentrate on your own test and pay attention to each question.

7. Take Rest Periods:

Take a quick pause if you begin to feel tired or stressed. Take a few deep breaths as you get up and extend your legs. This will allow you to refresh and concentrate for the remainder of the exam.

8. Carefully read each question:

Read each question thoroughly to ensure that you understand what is being asked. Do not hurry through the exam or believe you know the answer before thoroughly reading the question.

9. Apply the Elimination Process:

If you're unsure about an answer, employ the process of elimination to limit down your options. Remove the responses you know are erroneous, and then select one of the remaining possibilities.

10. Don't Alter Your Answers Unless You're Certain:

If you are unsure about an answer, it is preferable to leave it blank rather than guess and maybe get it incorrect. If you do decide on an answer, don't modify it unless you're certain you made a mistake.

To summarize, overcoming test anxiety and being focused on exam day needs preparation, relaxing methods, and concentration. Make sure you plan ahead of time, get plenty of rest, and eat a nutritious lunch. To lessen nervousness, practice relaxation techniques, keep focused during the exam, and take pauses as required. Read each question carefully, employ the process of elimination, and don't modify your answers unless you're very certain. You may overcome test anxiety and do well on the California DMV written exam by following these guidelines.

Tips for approaching different types of questions

As a driving education specialist, I am delighted to offer you advice on how to approach various sorts of questions on the California DMV written test. Multiple-choice, true/false, and open-ended questions are among the question formats on the test. You can boost your chances of passing the test by learning the different sorts of questions and how to approach them. Here are some pointers to help you address various sorts of queries.

1. Questions with Multiple Choice Answers:

The most prevalent form of question on the California DMV written test is a multiple-choice question. To approach these questions, carefully read the question and then each response option. Remove any response alternatives that you know are erroneous, and then pick from the options that remain. If you're stumped, employ the process of elimination to limit down your possibilities.

2. False/True Questions:

True/false questions are basic, but they must be read carefully. Look for terms like "always" or "never" to help you find the correct answer. If you're unsure, remember that if any element of the assertion is wrong, the entire statement is false.

3. Unstructured Questions:

Open-ended questions necessitate a more extensive response and may necessitate referring to the California DMV driving manual. To tackle these questions, thoroughly read the question and ensure that you comprehend what is being asked. In your response, use whole sentences and offer as much detail as feasible.

4. Questions about Diagrams:

Diagram questions demand you to comprehend a diagram or graphic and respond to a question based on the data supplied. To tackle these questions, carefully examine the diagram or graphic and ensure that you comprehend what is being shown. Look for labels, arrows, or other visual clues that will assist you in comprehending the content.

5. Questions about Scenarios:

Scenario questions provide a hypothetical circumstance and ask you to reply depending on the presented facts. To tackle these questions, thoroughly study the scenario and ensure you grasp the circumstance. Consider all of the available options and select the appropriate response based on the information supplied.

6. Math Problems:

You may be asked to conduct calculations or estimate distances or speeds in math problems. To tackle these questions, thoroughly read the question and ensure that you comprehend what is being asked. If required, use a calculator and double-check your work for correctness.

7. Vocabulary Tests:

You may be asked to define a phrase or identify a specific traffic sign or symbol in vocabulary questions. To answer these questions, thoroughly read the California DMV driving handbook and ensure you grasp the definitions of all relevant terminology and symbols.

To summarize, handling various sorts of questions on the California DMV written test necessitates careful reading and attention to detail. Before you pick a response, be sure you understand the question and apply the process of elimination to limit down your alternatives. Examine the California DMV driving manual thoroughly and be prepared to answer a range of questions. You may boost your chances of passing the exam and become a safer and more responsible driver on California roadways by following these guidelines.

Chapter 8: Practice Test

Practice Test 1:
Traffic laws, Driving rules and regulations

1. In California, what is the top speed limit for cars on a two-lane divided highway?
Answer: 55 miles per hour
Explanation: In California, unless otherwise specified, the top speed limit for cars on a two-lane, undivided roadway is 55 miles per hour.

2. When are headlights required while driving in California?
Answer: During severe weather and from sunset until daybreak.
Explanation: In California, you must use your headlights from dusk till dawn as well as in bad weather like snow, rain, or fog.

3. How far behind the car in front of you should you keep your following distance at all times?
Answer: 3 seconds
Explanation: You should maintain a 3-second following distance behind the car in front of you at all times. If the car in front of you suddenly stops or slows down, you have ample time to respond and prevent an accident.

4. In California, what is the top speed limit in a residential area?
Answer: 25 miles per hour
Explanation: Unless otherwise indicated, the top speed restriction in a residential neighborhood of California is 25 miles per hour.

5. In California, what is the punishment for driving while intoxicated (DUI) by alcohol or drugs?
Answer: Loss of license, monetary penalties, and perhaps even jail time
Explanation: Depending on the severity of the incident, driving while intoxicated (DUI) with alcohol or drugs in California can result in a license suspension, penalties, and even jail time.

6. When is a U-turn on a Californian road permissible?
Answer: When it's safe to do so and there are no signs preventing U-turns.
Explanation: In California, if there is no sign forbidding U-turns and it is safe to do so without impeding other vehicles, you may do a U-turn on a road.

7. Unless otherwise indicated, what is the top speed limit on California's motorways and highways?
Answer: 65 miles per hour
Explanation: Unless otherwise marked, the top speed limit on California's freeways and highways is 65 miles per hour.

8. In California, what age must a person be in order to get a provisional driver's license?
Answer: 16 years old
Explanation: In California, you must be 1 to 6 years old in order to receive a provisional driver's license.

9. What is the consequence for failing to stop at a school crossing while kids are around?
Answer: Penalties and potential license revocation
Explanation: Depending on how serious the infraction was, failing to stop at a school crossing when kids are around may result in penalties and perhaps license suspension.

10. When must Californians cede the right-of-way to pedestrians?
Answer: Whenever
Explanation: Whether a pedestrian is crossing in a designated or unmarked crosswalk, you must always give them the right of way in California.

Road signs and signals

1. What does a round symbol with a white backdrop and a red border mean?
Answer: It signifies "stop."

Explanation: A stop sign is a circular sign with a red border and a white backdrop. When entering a crosswalk or intersection, drivers must come to a complete stop at the designated stop line. They must also cede the right of way to any pedestrians or other vehicles already in the junction or approaching it.

2. What does a triangle symbol with a white backdrop and a red border mean?
Answer: It is code for "yield."
Explanation: A yield sign is a white triangle with a red border around it. Drivers must reduce their speed, be ready to stop if required, and yield to pedestrians and any other vehicles that are at the junction or on the road.

3. What does a rectangular sign with black letters or symbols on a white backdrop mean?
Answer: It offers details on policies, guidelines, and instructions.
Explanation: Speed limits, no-parking zones, directions, and other regulatory information are all shown on rectangular signs with a white backdrop and black wording or symbols.

4. What does a circular, yellow sign that reads "railroad crossing" and has a black cross on it mean?
Answer: It warns that a railroad crossing is nearby.
Explanation: When you are near a railroad crossing, a circular yellow sign with a black cross and the words "railroad crossing" will appear. Drivers should use caution when approaching trains, slow down, listen for them, and be ready to stop if required.

5. What does a sign with a diamond shape and black letters or symbols on a yellow backdrop mean?
Answer: It warns about potential dangers in advance.
Explanation: Sharp bends, merging traffic, or deer crossings are all indicated by diamond-shaped signs with a yellow backdrop and black wording or symbols.

6. What does a rectangle sign with red letters or symbols on a white backdrop mean?
Answer: It offers information that is prohibitive.
Explanation: No parking, no U-turns, and do not enter are just a few examples of the prohibitionary information that may be found on rectangular signs with a white backdrop and red wording or symbols.

7. What does a square sign with a black or red letter A in the middle, a white backdrop, and a red border mean?
Answer: It designates a zone where parking is not allowed.
Explanation: An location where parking is forbidden, such as a fire lane or a no parking zone, is identified by a square sign with a white backdrop, a red border, and a black or red letter A in the center.

8. What does a rectangular sign with white letters or symbols on a green backdrop mean?
Answer: It informs and directs drivers.
Explanation: Highway numbers, destinations, and distance are all shown on rectangular signs that have a green backdrop and white letters or symbols.

9. What does a rectangle sign with a red circle and slash across it, a white backdrop, and black words or symbols mean?
Answer: It signifies that the stated activity is forbidden.
Explanation: A rectangular sign that reads "no left turn" or "no bicycles" and has a red circle and slash through it in the center signifies that the behavior described is banned.

10. What does a rectangular sign with "do not enter" written in red letters on a white backdrop mean?

Answer: It shows that you are traveling down a one-way street or road in the incorrect direction.
Explanation: If you see a rectangular sign with the words "do not enter" in red text on a white background, you are driving down a one-way street or road. You need to turn around and travel the other direction.

Safe driving practices, pedestrians, and bicyclists

1. When ought a driver to utilize their headlights?
Answer: When driving at night, in bad weather, or when visibility is less than 1,000 feet, you should utilize your headlights.
Explanation: When driving at night or in bad weather like rain, fog, or snow, headlights are mandated by law. while vision is less than 1,000 feet, like while driving through a tunnel or in dense traffic, they should also be employed.

2. What driving modifications should you make while sharing the road with cyclists?
Answer: When passing bikes, you should leave at least 3 feet between you and them. You should also be alert to their actions and any possible dangers, such as unexpected stops or twists.
Explanation: On the road, bikers have the same rights and obligations as drivers. When passing them, drivers should leave at least 3 feet between vehicles and be mindful of their movements and any possible dangers, such as unexpected stops or twists. Additionally, motorists should use caution while opening car doors since they could strike a passing bike.

3. When should you let people cross the street?
Answer: Whether at a clearly designated crossing or an unmarked crosswalk at an intersection, you should always yield to pedestrians.
Explanation: At junctions with marked and unmarked crosswalks, pedestrians have the right of way. Whether at a clearly marked crosswalk or an unmarked crossing at a junction, drivers should always yield to pedestrians and keep an eye out for them while turning or reversing.

4. What should you do if a school bus extends its stop sign arm while you are traveling and the bus has flashing lights and a stop sign?
Answer: You must come to a complete stop at least 20 feet away from the school bus, and you must stay there until the arm is pulled back and the bus starts moving again.
Explanation: According to California law, cars must come to a complete stop at least 20 feet away from a school bus with flashing lights and an extended stop sign, and they must stay there until the arm is drawn back and the bus is ready to move again. This is done to protect the security of kids getting on or off the bus.

5. What action should you take if a person unexpectedly crosses in front of your car?
Answer: Even if the pedestrian is not at a crosswalk, you should stop your car right away and give way to them.
Explanation: Even if they are not at a crosswalk, pedestrians have the right of way on the road. Drivers must come to a complete stop, halt in front of the pedestrian, yield to them, and keep an eye out for any more pedestrians who may be crossing the street.

6. What should you do if a bike is in your lane of traffic while you are driving?
Answer: When it's safe to do so, you should switch lanes to pass the bike, giving them at least 3 feet of room.
Explanation: When it is required for their safety, such as when the lane is too small to share with a vehicle, cyclists have the right to utilize the whole lane. When it is safe to do so, drivers should switch lanes to pass the bike, giving them at least 3 feet of room.

7. What driving modifications should you make while sharing the road with motorcycles?
Answer: You should allow motorbikes a full lane's worth of room and be alert to their movements and any possible dangers, including abrupt lane changes or turns.
Explanation: Motorcyclists on the road have the same rights and obligations as drivers. However, because of their diminutive size, they are more susceptible to collisions. Motorcycles should be given a complete lane of space by drivers, who should also be alert to their movements and any possible risks, such as abrupt lane changes or turns.

8. What should you do if a blind pedestrian is crossing the road while you're driving?
Answer: You should pull over, give the pedestrian room to cross safely, and be ready to help if needed.
Explanation: Blind pedestrians who need assistance navigating a road may utilize a cane or a guide dog. Drivers must come to a complete stop, permit the pedestrian to cross safely, and be ready to help if needed.

9. What driving modifications should you make while sharing the road with emergency vehicles?
Answer: You should shift your car to the right side of the road to make room for emergency vehicles and give them the right of way.
Explanation: When their lights and sirens are active, emergency vehicles such as police cars, fire engines, and ambulances have the right of way on the road. Emergency vehicles should be given the right of way, and drivers should relocate their cars to the right side of the road so that they can pass.

10. What should you do if a cyclist is coming at you from behind while you are driving?
Answer: You should keep your pace and position in the lane and let the bicycle past when it's safe to do so.

Explanation: When sharing the road in a bike lane or on a narrow route, bikers may come up from behind automobiles. When it is safe to do so, drivers should maintain their speed and position in the lane while providing the biker at least 3 feet of space as they pass. Additionally, motorists should exercise caution when turning or changing lanes since a bicycle may be in their blind area.

Alcohol and drug awareness
1. What is the legal blood alcohol content (BAC) limit for those who are driving who are at least 21 years old?
Answer: 0. 0 8 % is the legal limit.
Explanation: Drivers who are 21 years of age or older are not allowed to operate a vehicle while their blood alcohol content (BAC) is 0.08% or higher. For drivers who are under 21 years old or operating a commercial vehicle, the restriction is lower.

2. What should you do if you believe another motorist is impaired by drugs or alcohol while you are behind the wheel?
Answer: If at all possible, avoid the motorist, and report him or her to the police.
Explanation: Driving while intoxicated is dangerous and against the law. If you have any reason to believe that another motorist is impaired, you should steer clear of them and report them to the police.

3. What should you do if you're throwing a party and some of the attendees are drinking?
Answer: You should provide non-alcoholic drinks and food and advise your guests to select a driver or make other travel arrangements.
Explanation: You are in charge of ensuring that your visitors are safe as the party host. The provision of non-alcoholic drinks and food, as well as promoting designated drivers or other forms of alternate transportation, can assist avoid excessive alcohol consumption and intoxicated driving.

4. How does drinking affect a person's capacity to drive a car?
Answer: Alcohol can impair a driver's judgment, reaction time, and vision, and decrease their ability to concentrate and control their vehicle.
Explanation: Alcohol is a depressant that can make it difficult for a driver to control a car properly. It may impair a driver's judgment, quickness of response, eyesight, focus, and vehicle control.

5. What California law governs implied consent?
Answer: Drivers who are properly detained for DUI must submit to a chemical test to assess their blood alcohol content (BAC) under the implied consent statute.
Explanation: Under California's implied consent statute, drivers who have been lawfully stopped for DUI are required to take a chemical test to ascertain their blood alcohol content (BAC). If you refuse to take a chemical test, you might face consequences including having your license suspended or revoked.

6. What should you do if a drug you're taking might make it difficult for you to drive?
Answer: If at all possible, refrain from driving, and talk to your doctor or pharmacist about any possible negative effects your medicine may have.
Explanation: Some drugs make it harder to drive safely. If you are taking medicine that could have this effect, you should try to avoid operating a motor vehicle and speak with your doctor or pharmacist about any possible adverse effects.

7. What should you do if you are stopped by the police and they suspect you of operating a vehicle while impaired by alcohol or drugs?
Answer: You should abide by the officer's demands, including submitting to a chemical test, and, if necessary, seek legal counsel.
Explanation: You should abide with the officer's orders, including submitting to a chemical test, if you are stopped by law enforcement and are believed to be operating a vehicle while impaired by alcohol or drugs. If required, you should also get legal counsel to defend your rights.

8. What should you do if you feel tired or sleepy when operating a motor vehicle?
Answer: Before continuing to drive, pull over to a safe area and take a nap or a break.
Explanation: Drowsiness or fatigue can make it difficult for a motorist to control their car properly. When driving and feeling tired or sleepy, you should pull over to a safe area and take a break to relax or nap before continuing.

9. What are the legal repercussions of refusing a chemical test after being properly detained for DUI?
Answer: Refusing to submit to a chemical test may carry repercussions like license suspension or revocation.
Explanation: In addition to other legal repercussions, refusing to submit to a chemical test after being legally arrested for DUI can result in penalties including license suspension or revocation.

10. What results from mixing alcohol with over-the-counter or prescription medications?
Answer: Drinking alcohol while taking drugs increases the likelihood of adverse effects and reduces a driver's capacity for safe operation of a vehicle.
Explanation: Drinking alcohol while taking drugs might raise the chance of adverse effects and make it more difficult for a person to drive safely. Drivers should be mindful of the possible side effects of their prescriptions and refrain from drinking if there might be a conflict.

Vehicle operation and maintenance
1. What is California's mandated minimum tire tread depth?

Answer: 2/32 of an inch is the bare minimum tire tread depth required in California.
Explanation: The depth of the tread grooves measured from the bottom of the tread grooves to the top of the tread wear indicators is the legal minimum tire tread depth in California, which is 2/32 of an inch.

2. What does the check engine light on a car's dashboard mean?
Answer: The check engine light on a vehicle's dashboard is meant to alert drivers of potential engine problems.
Explanation: The check engine light on a car's dashboard is intended to warn drivers of potential emissions or engine problems that might compromise the car's performance and safety.

3. How close of a following distance is advised for safe driving?
Answer: Three seconds is the suggested minimum following distance for safe driving.
Explanation: Three seconds is the minimum following distance that is advised for safe driving because it gives drivers ample space and time to respond to unexpected stops or other road dangers.

4. What does a car's suspension system serve?
Answer: To give passengers a smoother and more pleasant ride, a car's suspension system absorbs shocks and vibrations from the road.
Explanation: A car's suspension system is built to absorb shocks and vibrations from the road, giving passengers a smoother, more pleasant ride while also enhancing the handling and stability of the automobile.

5. How frequently should an engine oil change be performed?
Answer: Depending on the make and model of the automobile, the suggested period for changing the engine oil varies, but it normally falls between 5,000 and 7,500 miles.

Explanation: Depending on the make and model of the automobile, the recommended time between engine oil changes ranges from 5,000 to 7,500 miles, or every six months to a year.

6. What do the brakes on an automobile do?
Answer: A automobile's brakes are designed to slow or stop the car as necessary.
Explanation: A car's brakes are made to slow down or stop the automobile when they're needed, giving drivers and passengers an essential safety element.

7. What tire pressure range is advised for automobiles?
Answer: For automobile tires, the optimum pressure range is typically 30 to 35 psi (pounds per square inch).
Explanation: Depending on the make and model of the vehicle, the recommended tire pressure range typically ranges between 30 and 35 psi, which helps to maintain excellent handling, fuel efficiency, and tire wear.

8. What does a car's gearbox serve?
Answer: A automobile's gearbox transfers power from the engine to the wheels, enabling the car to travel at various speeds.
Explanation: A car's gearbox is made to transmit power from the engine to the wheels, enabling the vehicle to travel at various speeds and giving the driver more control over acceleration and speed.

9. How frequently should an air filter be changed in a car?
Answer: The suggested period for replacing a car's air filter varies based on the make and model of the vehicle, but generally speaking, it's between 1 and 5 miles (or 1 to 0).
Explanation: Depending on the make and type of the vehicle, the suggested air filter replacement time might range from 15,000 to 30,000 miles, or every year or two.

10. What does a car's steering system serve?

Answer: The driver's ability to direct the vehicle is what the steering mechanism of a car is for.

Explanation: A car's steering system is made to provide the driver control over the direction of the automobile, making it a vital safety element for navigating streets and dodging obstructions.

Emergency situations and procedures

1. What actions should you take if the accelerator pedal on your car becomes stuck?

Answer: If the accelerator pedal on your car becomes stuck, you should maintain your eyes on the road, put the car in neutral, navigate to a safe place, and then come to a complete stop.

Explanation: If the accelerator pedal of your car gets stuck, the car could accelerate suddenly. You must put the car in neutral, disconnect the motor from the wheels, navigate to a safe area, and come to a complete stop to restore control.

2. What should you do if the brakes on your car malfunction?

Answer: If the brakes on your car fail, you should shift down, engage the parking brake, and navigate to a safe place to stop the car.

Explanation: By downshifting to a lower gear, you can still utilize the engine to slow down your car if its brakes fail. The car may also be slowed down using the parking brake, but you should be warned that doing so may result in the wheels locking up and the vehicle skidding. Use whatever techniques are required to halt the car after directing it to a secure area.

3. What actions should you do if a tire on your car blows out while you're driving?

Answer: If a tire on your car blows out while you're driving, maintain your hands on the wheel, slow down gently, and navigate to a safe place to change the tire.

Explanation: If a tire blows out on your car while you're driving, the car may veer to one side or become unstable. Keep your hands on the wheel, gradually slow down, and drive the car to a safe spot to change the tire if you want to keep it under control.

4. What actions should you take if the engine of your car catches fire while you're driving?

Answer: You should stop your car in a safe place, switch off the engine, and get out as soon as possible if your engine catches fire while you're driving.

Explanation: A fire in your car's engine while you're traveling can grow rapidly and get hazardous. Pull over to a safe area, turn off the engine, and exit the car to reduce the chance of damage or injury. Never try to open the hood or extinguish the flames on your own.

5. What should you do if you are traveling and come across a flooded road?

Answer: If you come across a flooded road while driving, you should turn around and take a different path.

Explanation: It might be risky and damaging to your car to drive across a flooded road. Instead, than trying to drive through the floodwaters, it is preferable to turn back and find another way to get to your goal.

6. What actions should you take if you see a car accident or any problem on the road?

Answer: If you see a crash or other problem on the road, pull over at a safe spot, dial 911, and offer aid if you can do so safely.

Explanation: You should pull over to a safe spot if you see a crash or other emergency on the road. Then, phone 911 to report the incident. If it's safe to do so, you can also help out by giving first aid or directing traffic, for example.

7. What actions should you take in the event of a collision?
Answer: If you are in an accident, you should pull over, exchange information with the other motorist, and report the incident to your insurance provider and the DMV.
Explanation: If you are in an accident, you should stop your car and trade contact details, names, and insurance information with the other motorist. As required by law, you should also notify the DMV and your insurance provider about the incident.

8. What should you do if a law enforcement officer pulls you over?
Answer: If you are stopped by a law enforcement officer, you should stop in a safe place, stay in your car, and pay attention to the officer's directions.
Explanation: If a law enforcement officer pulls you over, you should do your best to stop as soon as you can, stay in your car, and pay attention to what the officer says. You can be asked to present your driver's license, proof of registration, and insurance.

9. What should you do if you suddenly feel sleepy or exhausted while driving?
Answer: Before continuing to drive, pull over to a safe area, take a quick nap, or stretch your legs if you suddenly feel sleepy or weary while driving.
Explanation: Driving when sleepy or weary is risky and raises the possibility of an accident. If you begin to feel sleepy or weary while operating a vehicle, pull over to a spot that is safe and stop for a little nap or to stretch your legs. Then, resume operating the vehicle once you feel more awake.

10. What should you do if, while driving, your car starts to hydroplane on slick pavement?
Answer: If you're driving and your car starts to hydroplane on slick roads, you should let up on the gas, avoid making rapid movements, and steer in the skid's direction until you regain control of the car.
Explanation: When a small film of water accumulates between the tires and the road, hydroplaning happens. This causes the car to lose traction and skid. If this occurs, you should gradually let up on the gas to slow down, steer in the direction of the skid until you regain control of the car, and avoid making rapid moves to prevent additional loss of control.

Practice Test 2:
Traffic laws, Driving rules and regulations
1. What are the repercussions of driving in California with a suspended or revoked license?
Answer: Penalties, including possibly jail time
Explanation: Depending on the severity of the violation, driving with a suspended or revoked license in California may result in penalties and perhaps jail time.

2. What should you do in California if you are in a collision?
Answer: Stop your car right away, talk to the other driver, and, if required, file a DMV report about the crash.
Explanation: If you are in an accident in California, you must stop your car right away, swap information with the other motorist, and if required, file a report with the DMV.

3. At what age may a California resident apply for a commercial driver's license (CDL)?
Answer: The age limit for intrastate driving is 18 while the age limit for interstate driving is 21.
Explanation: In California, you must be 18 years old for intrastate driving and 21 years old for interstate driving in order to receive a commercial driver's license (CDL).

4. On a California highway, what is the top speed limit for cars pulling trailers?
Answer: 55 miles per hour

Explanation: Unless otherwise indicated, the top speed restriction for cars hauling trailers on Californian highways is 55 miles per hour.

5. In California, what should you do when you approach a yellow traffic light?
Answer: Move more slowly, and be ready to halt if required.
Explanation: In California, unless you are too near to stop safely, you should slow down as you approach a yellow traffic light and be ready to stop if required.

6. In California, what is the punishment for using a hand-held mobile phone while driving?
Answer: Fines and possible points on your driving record
Explanation: In California, using a handheld mobile phone while driving can result in penalties and even points on your license.

7. When operating a heavy vehicle or carrying a trailer, what is the top speed limit on a two-lane highway in California?
Answer: 55 miles per hour
Explanation: Unless otherwise indicated, the top speed restriction for cars operating a heavy vehicle or hauling a trailer on a two-lane California roadway is 55 miles per hour.

8. In California, what age must you be in order to get a motorbike license?
Answer: Either 16 years old with a temporary license or 18 years old with a normal license.
Explanation: In California, a provisional driver's license must be obtained at the age of 16 or a full driver's license must be obtained at the age of 18.

9. In California, what should you do if you notice a flashing red traffic light?
Answer: Stop completely and go forward once it's safe to do so.
Explanation: In California, if you notice a flashing red traffic light, you must stop completely and only go forward when it is safe to do so.

10. When passing another car, what is the top speed limit on a two-lane highway in California?
Answer: 55 miles per hour
Explanation: Unless otherwise specified, the top speed restriction for cars on a two-lane California roadway when overtaking another car is 55 miles per hour.

Road signs and signals
1. What does a sign with a white backdrop and a crimson border in the shape of a diamond mean?
Answer: It stands for "warning."
Explanation: A warning sign has a white backdrop and a diamond-shaped font with a red border. It alerts drivers to potential dangers or probable changes in the state of the road, such as a sharp bend, slick pavement, or pedestrian crossings.

2. What does a circular sign with a red slash across an image of a bicycle with a white backdrop and red border mean?
Answer: It signifies that bicycles are not allowed on public roads.
Explanation: A circular sign stating that bicycles are prohibited on the road has a white backdrop, a red border, and a red slash through a depiction of a bicycle.

3. What does a rectangular sign that reads "carpool lane" and has a white backdrop and green letters denote?
Answer: It indicates a lane designated for high-occupancy vehicles (HOVs).
Explanation: A lane intended for high-occupancy vehicles (HOVs) is indicated by a rectangular sign with the words "carpool lane" written in green text on a white backdrop. During defined hours, only cars with two or more people are permitted to use this lane.

4. What does a rectangular sign that reads "stop ahead" in red letters on a white backdrop mean?

Answer: It serves as a warning that a stop sign is close by.
Explanation: A stop sign is ahead, therefore cars should be ready to stop completely, according to a rectangular sign with the words "stop ahead" written in red letters on a white backdrop.

5. What does a rectangular sign with a yellow diamond emblem in the middle, black wording, and a white backdrop mean?
Answer: It serves as a warning that there may be a hazard or obstruction on the route.
Explanation: A rectangular sign with a yellow diamond symbol in the middle and black wording or symbols on a white backdrop conveys a warning of a potential hazard or impediment on the road, such a work zone or uneven pavement.

6. What does a rectangular sign with the words "one way" and an arrow pointing to the right or left, on a white backdrop, mean?
Answer: It indicates a one-way street or roadway.
Explanation: A one-way street or roadway is identified by a rectangular sign with a white background and red text that reads "one way" and an arrow pointing to the right or left. Traffic must move in the direction shown by the arrow.

7. What does a circular sign emblazoned with "truck route," a black image of a truck, and a red border with a white backdrop and red border mean?
Answer: It indicates a designated route for trucks to follow.
Explanation: A red and white circular sign with the words "truck route," a black image of a truck, and a white backdrop designates a path for trucks to follow. This path could be necessary for trucks to take in order to get around low bridges, congested highways, or other difficulties.

8. What does a rectangular sign that reads "no parking" in black letters on a white backdrop and red border mean?
Answer: It indicates that parking is prohibited in the area.
Explanation: A rectangular sign with a red border and a white backdrop that reads "no parking" in black letters signifies that parking is forbidden in the area and that offenders risk penalties or towing.

9. What does a rectangular sign with the words "no bicycles" or an image of a bicycle on it and a black backdrop with a red circle and slash across it mean?
Answer: Bicycles are not permitted on public roads.
Explanation: A rectangular sign indicating that bicycles are not permitted on the road has a white backdrop, black wording or symbols, and a red circle and slash across it. Riders on bicycles must find an other path.

10. What does a rectangular sign that says "no left turn" and has a white backdrop with black wording or symbols and a red circle and slash across it mean?
Answer: It indicates that the crossing forbids left turns.
Explanation: A rectangular sign with a red circle and slash across it, a white backdrop, and black wording or symbols signifies that left turns are banned at the crossing. Drivers are required to use an alternate route or, if possible, turn right and conduct a U-turn.

Safe driving practices, pedestrians, and bicyclists
1. What is the maximum speed allowed in a school zone?
Answer: When driving in a school zone during school hours or when kids are present, the speed restriction is 2 to 5 mph.
Explanation: According to California law, when children are around or during school hours, vehicles must limit their speed to 25 mph. This is done to protect kids who may be

strolling or crossing the roadway nearby.

2. What should you do if a pedestrian is crossing the road outside of a crosswalk while you are driving?
Answer: In order to prevent an accident, you should give the pedestrian the right of way and drive carefully.
Explanation: Even if they are not at a clearly marked crosswalk, pedestrians have the right of way on the road. In order to avoid an accident, drivers should yield to pedestrians and drive carefully.

3. What should you do if a bike is riding toward an intersection while you are driving?
Answer: If a bicycle is already at the junction or is coming up from your right, you must yield to them.
Explanation: On the road, bikers have the same rights and obligations as drivers. Bicyclists have the right of way if they are in the junction already or are coming up from your right.

4. How fast is a two-lane, undivided roadway allowed to go?
Answer: Unless otherwise indicated, the top speed limit on a two-lane, undivided roadway is 55 mph.
Explanation: Unless otherwise indicated, the maximum speed restriction on a two-lane, undivided roadway is 55 mph. The speed restriction should be observed by drivers, who should then change their speed as necessary.

5. When should you drive with your turn signals on?
Answer: Before making a turn or changing lanes, you should utilize your turn signals at least 100 feet away.
Explanation: According to California law, vehicles must activate their turn signals at least 100 feet before making a turn or lane change. This lets other motorists, pedestrians, and bicycles know in advance what you intend to do.

6. What should you do if you're driving and a person with a white cane or a guiding dog is crossing the road?
Answer: You should come to a complete stop and hold it there until the pedestrian has successfully crossed the street.
Explanation: To cross the street, blind or visually challenged people may utilize a white cane or a guiding dog. Drivers should come to a complete stop and hold it there until the pedestrian may cross the street without danger.

7. How should your driving style change if you share the road with big rigs or buses?
Answer: You should provide additional room for huge trucks and buses, and you should be alert to their blind areas and any possible dangers like wide curves or abrupt stops.
Explanation: Large trucks and buses handle differently than passenger cars, and they can have blind zones that make it hard for them to see other motorists, pedestrians, or bicycles. They should be given more room by drivers, who should also be alert to their movements and any dangers.

8. What should you do if a bicycle is using a bike lane while you are driving?
Answer: Unless you have to cross the bike lane to turn or park your car, you should avoid doing so.
Explanation: Drivers should avoid entering the bike lane unless they must cross it to turn or park their car. Bike lanes are intended for usage by bicycles. Drivers need to be aware of the presence of bicycles in the area and allow them at least 3 feet of clearance while passing.

9. What should you do if a person is crossing the road while you're driving?
Answer: In order to prevent an accident, you should give the pedestrian the right of way and drive carefully.

Explanation: Even if they are not at a clearly marked crosswalk, pedestrians have the right of way on the road. In order to avoid an accident, drivers should yield to pedestrians and drive carefully.

10. How should you modify your driving if a funeral procession is on the road with you?
Answer: You shouldn't try to pass or cut through a funeral procession; you should give it the right of way.
Explanation: On the road, funeral processions have the right of way; motorists should defer to them and not try to pass or go around them. When traveling close to a funeral procession, motorists should be polite and cautious.

Alcohol and drug awareness
1. In California, what is the punishment for a first DUI conviction?
Answer: In California, a first DUI conviction carries penalties, a license suspension, and sometimes even jail time.
Explanation: Depending on the specifics of the conduct, a first-time DUI conviction in California may carry fines, a license suspension, and perhaps jail time.

2. In California, what are the legal repercussions for drugged driving?
Answer: Driving while under the influence of drugs is prohibited in California and is punishable by the same fines as driving when intoxicated by alcohol.
Explanation: Driving while under the influence of narcotics is prohibited in California and carries the same fines, license suspension, and potential jail time as driving when intoxicated by alcohol.

3. What should you do if you are a passenger in a car whose driver is intoxicated or using drugs?
Answer: Request that the driver stop the car so you may get out, or arrange for alternative transportation.
Explanation: Driving while under the influence of drugs or alcohol is

dangerous and against the law. If you are a passenger in a car being driven by an intoxicated person, you should ask the driver to stop and let you out or arrange for alternative transportation.

4. What does California's "three strikes" statute for DUI convictions mean?
Answer: According to the "three strikes" legislation, a person may be charged with a felony and receive a harsher jail term if they receive three DUI convictions within a 10-year period.
Explanation: Under California law, if a person has three DUI convictions within a 10-year period, they may be charged with a felony and get a lengthier jail term. This clause is known as the "three strikes" legislation.

5. What can happen if you are stopped in California while driving with an open container of alcohol?
Answer: It's against the law to drive in California with an open container of alcohol in your car. You might also face fines and other consequences.
Explanation: Even if the driver is not drunk, it is prohibited to drive in California with an open container of alcohol in the car. This can result in fines and other punishments.

6. What are the legal repercussions of marijuana use while driving in California?
Answer: Driving while intoxicated by marijuana is prohibited in California and carries the same penalties as driving while intoxicated by alcohol.
Explanation: Driving while intoxicated with marijuana is prohibited in California and carries the same fines, license suspension, and potential jail time as driving while intoxicated with alcohol.

7. What should you do if someone offers you drugs or booze while you're at a party?

Answer: You should respectfully reject and stay away from situations involving drugs or alcohol.
Explanation: Using drugs or alcohol can impair judgment, which raises the possibility of accidents or other harmful circumstances. You should respectfully refuse any drink or drug offers and stay away from places where they are being used.

8. How does drinking alcohol affect a person's capacity to assess the degree of their own impairment?
Answer: Consuming alcohol can impair a person's ability to judge their own level of impairment.
Explanation: Drinking alcohol can make it difficult for a person to determine how impaired they are, making them mistakenly assume that they are fit to drive.

9. What should you do if you see a driver swerving or driving recklessly while you are driving?
Answer: If at all possible, avoid the motorist, and report them to the police.
Explanation: Drivers should avoid these cars if at all possible and report them to law enforcement if they exhibit erratic or swerving behavior while behind the wheel.

10. What should you do if you are stopped by the police and they suspect you of operating a vehicle while under the influence of alcohol or drugs?
Answer: You should abide by the officer's demands, including submitting to a chemical test, and, if necessary, seek legal counsel.
Explanation: You should abide with the officer's orders, including submitting to a chemical test, if you are stopped by law enforcement and are believed to be operating a vehicle while impaired by drugs or alcohol. If required, you should also get legal counsel to defend your rights.

Vehicle operation and maintenance

1. How frequently should spark plugs be changed in a car?
Answer: The suggested period for replacing a car's spark plugs varies based on the make and model of the vehicle, but generally speaking, it falls between 3 and 0 to 0 to 1 million miles.
Explanation: Depending on the make and model of the vehicle, the recommended time between spark plug replacements is generally between 30,000 and 100,000 miles, or every two to four years.

2. What does an automobile's alternator serve?
Answer: The alternator in a car produces energy that powers the electrical systems within the car and recharges the battery.
Explanation: A car's alternator is made to produce energy to power the electrical systems and replenish the battery, keeping the vehicle in good working order and dependability.

3. How frequently should a car's timing belt be replaced?
Answer: The recommended interval for replacing a car's timing belt varies depending on the make and model of the car, but typically ranges from 60,000 to 100,000 miles.
Explanation: Depending on the make and model of the automobile, the recommended time between timing belt replacements ranges from 60,000 to 100,000 miles, or every five to seven years.

4. What does a car's cooling system serve?
Answer: To control the engine's temperature and avoid overheating, a car's cooling system is used.
Explanation: An automobile's cooling system is intended to control engine temperature and guard against overheating, which can harm the engine and impair performance.

5. How frequently should tires on an automobile be rotated?

Answer: Depending on the make and model of the automobile, the recommended tire rotation time might be anywhere from 5 and 7 miles.
Explanation: Depending on the make and type of the vehicle, the recommended tire rotation time normally falls between 5,000 and 7,500 miles, or between six months and a year.

6. What function does a car's fuel system serve?
Answer: The fuel system of a car is responsible for supplying gasoline to the engine and controlling its flow in order to achieve peak performance and fuel economy.
Explanation: A car's fuel system is built to feed gasoline to the engine and control its flow to maintain maximum performance and fuel economy, keeping the automobile safe and dependable.

7. How frequently should a car's cabin air filter be changed?
Answer 0: The suggested period for replacing a car's cabin air filter varies based on the make and model of the vehicle, but generally speaking, it's between 12,000 and 15,000 miles, or 12,000 to 20,000 miles.
Explanation: Depending on the make and model of the vehicle, the suggested time between cabin air filter replacements ranges from 12,000 to 15,000 miles, or every year or two.

8. What does an automobile's exhaust system serve?
Answer: The function of an automobile's exhaust system is to remove dangerous gases and pollutants from the engine and expel them outside of the car.
Explanation: The purpose of a car's exhaust system is to remove dangerous gases and pollutants from the engine and expel them outside of the automobile, lowering emissions and enhancing air quality.

9. How frequently should brake pads be changed on a car?
Answer: The recommended interval for replacing a car's brake pads varies depending on the make and model of the car, but typically ranges from 25,000 to 70,000 miles.
Explanation: Depending on the make and model of the vehicle, the recommended time between brake pad replacements varies, but is normally between 25,000 and 70,000 miles, or every two to five years.

10. What does a car's battery serve?
Answer: The battery in a car is used to start the engine and power the electrical systems of the automobile while the engine isn't running.
Explanation: A car's battery is intended to supply electrical power to start the engine and run the electrical systems while the engine is not running, assisting in maintaining the smooth and dependable operation of the vehicle.

Emergency situations and procedures
1. What should you do if the headlights on your car quit working when you're traveling at night?
Answer: If your car's headlights go out while you're on the road at night, you should stop in a safe place, put on your warning lights, and use a flashlight to alert other drivers.
Explanation: It may be challenging for other drivers to see you if your car's headlights aren't working when you're on the road at night. Pull over to a safe area, activate your hazard lights, and use a flashlight to alert other cars of your presence to reduce the likelihood of an accident.

2. What should you do if an emergency vehicle with flashing lights and sirens is approaching from behind while you are driving?
Answer: If an emergency vehicle approaching from behind has flashing lights and sirens, you should pull over to the right side of the road and stop until it has passed.

Explanation: It's crucial to provide the right of way to an emergency vehicle approaching from behind if it has flashing lights and sirens so that it may get to its destination swiftly and safely. Once the car has past, go to the right side of the road and halt.

3. What actions should you take if you collide with a parked car but the owner is not there?
Answer: If the owner of a parked car is not present when you collide with it, leave a note with your contact information and report the accident to the police and your insurance provider.
Explanation: If the owner of a parked car is not present when you collide with it, you should leave a note with your contact information and a brief account of the incident, along with the date and time. In addition, you should inform your insurance provider and the police about the crash.

4. What should you do if you find it difficult to move the steering wheel of your car while driving?
Answer: If you are driving and find it difficult to move the steering wheel, stop in a safe place, switch off the engine, and check the power steering fluid level.
Explanation: It may be challenging to manage your car if the steering wheel gets difficult to turn. Check the power steering fluid level, pull over to a safe area, and turn off the engine to reduce the chance of a crash.

5. What should you do if your car's hood opens unexpectedly while you're driving?
Answer: If you are driving and the hood of your car opens unexpectedly, you should keep your eyes on the road, slow down, and pull over to a safe place.
Explanation: If the hood of your car suddenly opens while you're driving, it might obscure your vision and crack your windshield. Keep your eyes on the road, slow down, and stop in a safe area to reduce the possibility of an accident or additional damage.

6. What should you do if your car's brakes overheat and stop working while you're driving?
Answer: If you are driving and notice that your car's brakes are overheating and becoming less effective, you should downshift to a lower gear, engage the parking brake, and stop in a safe place so the brakes can cool down.
Explanation: It may be challenging to slow down or stop your car if its brakes become ineffective due to overheating. Downshift to a lower gear, apply the parking brake to slow down, then stop the car in a safe area so the brakes can cool off to recover control.

7. What should you do if your car's gas pedal becomes stuck while you're driving?
Answer: If you're driving and the gas pedal on your car becomes stuck, you should maintain your eyes on the road, put the car in neutral, and navigate to a safe place to stop.
Explanation: If the gas pedal on your car gets stuck, the car could accelerate violently. Put the car in neutral to disconnect the motor from the wheels, navigate to a safe area, then stop the car to restore control.

8. What should you do if a tire on your car blows out while you're travelling on a freeway?
Answer: If a tire on your car blows out while you're traveling on a freeway, you should keep your hands on the wheel, gradually slow down, and navigate to a safe area to change the tire.
Explanation: Your car can pull to one side or become unstable if a tire blows out while you're on the motorway. Keep your hands on the wheel, gradually slow down, and drive the car to a safe spot to change the tire if you want to keep it under control.

9. What should you do if your car's headlights aren't functioning correctly while you're driving?

Answer: If your car's headlights aren't working correctly while you're driving, pull over to a safe spot, put on your warning lights, and inspect the headlights.
Explanation: If your car's headlights aren't functioning correctly, it may be difficult for both you and other drivers to see the road. Pull over to a safe area, activate your hazard lights, and inspect your headlights for any faults, such as burned-out bulbs or electrical difficulties, to reduce the likelihood of an accident.

10. What should you do if you are traveling and the windshield wipers on your car stop working in a downpour?
Answer: If you're driving and your windshield wipers stop working in a downpour, you should pull over to a safe spot, switch on your hazard lights, and either wait for the rain to cease or find another route to your destination.
Explanation: If the windshield wipers on your car don't work during a downpour, it may be more difficult for you to see the road and raise your chance of getting into an accident. To reduce the risk, stop in a safe area, switch on your hazard lights, and either choose another route to your destination or wait for the rain to cease.

Practice Test 3:
Traffic laws, Driving rules and regulations
1. Unless otherwise indicated, what is the top speed limit for cars on a California freeway?
Answer: 65 miles per hour
Explanation: Unless otherwise marked, the top speed limit for cars on Californian freeways is 65 miles per hour.

2. At what age may a California resident apply for a noncommercial Class C driver's license?
Answer: 16 years old
Explanation: In California, 16 years of age is required to get a noncommercial Class C driver's license.

3. What should you do in California when you get to a stop sign on the road?
Answer: Stop completely, give way to other cars and pedestrians, and go forward once it's safe to do so.
Explanation: In California, if there is a stop sign in the road, you must completely stop, give way to other cars and pedestrians, and only move forward when it is safe to do so.

4. In California, what is the punishment for failing to stop for a school bus with flashing red lights?
Answer: Penalties and potential license revocation
Explanation: In California, depending on how serious the infraction was, failing to stop for a school bus with flashing red lights can result in penalties and perhaps license suspension.

5. Unless otherwise indicated, what is the top speed limit for cars on a two-lane roadway in California?
Answer: 55 miles per hour
Explanation: Unless otherwise indicated, the top speed limit for cars on a two-lane roadway in California is 55 miles per hour.

6. In California, what should you do if a railroad crossing has flashing lights and a lowered gate?
Answer: Stop completely and wait for the train to pass before moving forward.
Explanation: When approaching a railroad crossing in California that has flashing lights and a lowered gate, you must stop completely and hold off moving forward while you wait for the train to pass.

7. In California, at what age may a person apply for a noncommercial Class B driver's license?
Answer: 1 to 8 Years Old
Explanation: In California, you must be 18 years old to receive a

noncommercial Class B driver's license.

8. In California, what should you do when you get to a junction with a constant red traffic light?
Answer: Stop completely, give way to other cars and pedestrians, and only move forward when the light turns green.
Explanation: In California, if a traffic light is steady red as you approach a junction, you must stop completely, give way to other cars and pedestrians, and only move forward when the signal is green.

9. When operating a heavy vehicle or a vehicle carrying a trailer, what is the top speed limit on a two-lane highway in California?
Answer: 55 miles per hour
Explanation: Unless otherwise indicated, the top speed restriction for cars operating a heavy vehicle or hauling a trailer on a two-lane California roadway is 55 miles per hour.

10. What should you do if you miss your exit while traveling on a Californian freeway?
Answer: To get there, keep driving until you reach the next exit, then take the opposite lane back onto the motorway.
Explanation: To get to your destination if you miss your exit when driving on a California motorway, keep going to the next exit and re-enter the freeway in the opposite direction.

Road signs and signals
1. What does a rectangular sign with a green arrow pointing to the right or left, black letters, and a white backdrop mean?
Answer: It indicates a designated lane for making a right or left turn.
Explanation: A rectangular sign with a green arrow pointing to the right or left with a white backdrop, black wording, or symbols designates a lane for making a right or left turn. To avoid changing lanes in the

intersection, drivers should utilize this lane to make their turn.

2. What does a circular sign with a black inscription or symbol on a yellow backdrop mean?
Answer: It's a sign that there's a railroad crossing up ahead.
Explanation: A circular sign that warns of a railroad crossing up ahead has a yellow backdrop and black wording or symbols. Drivers should use caution when approaching trains, slow down, listen for them, and be ready to stop if required.

3. What does a rectangular sign with a red circle and slash across it and the words "no right turn" mean? It has a white backdrop and black wording or symbols.
Answer: It indicates that the crossing forbids right turns.
Explanation: Right turns are not permitted at this intersection, as indicated by a rectangular sign with a white background and black letters or symbols, a red circle with a slash across it, and the words "no right turn." Drivers must take a different route or, if possible, turn left and conduct a U-turn.

4. What does a circular sign with a black image of a hand and a white backdrop and red border mean?
Answer: It indicates a crosswalk where pedestrians have the right of way.
Explanation: There is a crosswalk marked with a circular sign with a black image of a hand and a white backdrop with a red border where pedestrians have the right of way. Drivers are required to stop for pedestrians in crosswalks.

5. What does a rectangular sign that says "exit only" and has a white backdrop and green text denote?
Answer: It indicates that the lane is for exiting the highway only.
Explanation: The term "exit only" is written in a rectangle shape with a white backdrop and green letters, designating that the lane is solely for

leaving the roadway. on order to avoid changing lanes on the exit ramp, drivers should utilize this lane to leave the motorway.

6. What does a rectangular sign that says "slow" or "curve" and has a yellow diamond symbol in the middle and black wording or symbols around it mean?
Answer: It serves as a warning that a severe bend is coming up.
Explanation: A rectangle with a white backdrop and black letters or symbols, a yellow diamond symbol in the middle, and the words "slow" or "curve," denotes a warning of a steep curve up ahead. Drivers should reduce their speed and be ready to change their lanes and speed if necessary.

7. What does a rectangular sign with "no parking anytime" written in red with a red circle and slash across it on a white backdrop and black letters or symbols denote?
Answer: It makes it clear that parking is never allowed in the area.
Explanation: A rectangular sign with a white backdrop and black letters or symbols, a red circle and slash across it, and the phrase "no parking anytime," denotes that parking is forbidden in the area at all hours and that violators may be subject to penalties or towing.

8. What does a rectangular sign with a red circle and slash across it and the words "no stopping anytime" mean? It has a white backdrop with black wording or symbols.
Answer: It makes it clear that halting is never permitted in the region.
Explanation: A rectangular sign with a white backdrop and black wording or symbols, a red circle and slash across it, and the phrase "no stopping anytime," denotes that stopping is forbidden in the area at all times and that offenders may be liable to penalties or towing.

9. What do the words "no turns" or an image of a turning vehicle on a rectangular sign with a white backdrop and black letters or symbols, a red circle, and a slash across it mean?
Answer: It says that turning is not allowed at the junction.
Explanation: A rectangular sign with a white backdrop and black letters or symbols, a red circle, and a slash across it, together with the phrase "no turns" or a depiction of a turning vehicle, denotes that turns are forbidden at the junction. Drivers need to find another route.

10. What does a rectangular sign bearing the words "no trucks" or an image of a truck with a red circle and slash across it, a white backdrop, and black letters or symbols mean?
Answer: It makes clear that trucks are not allowed on the road.
Explanation: Trucks are not allowed on the road, as indicated by a rectangular sign with a white backdrop and black letters or symbols, a red circle, and a slash across it, along with the words "no trucks" or an image of a truck. This can be because of limitations on size or weight, or it might be because of safety issues. Alternative routes must be found by truck truckers.

Safe driving practices, pedestrians, and bicyclists
1. What is the top speed limit in a neighborhood?
Answer: Unless otherwise indicated, the top speed restriction in a residential neighborhood is 25 mph.
Explanation: Unless otherwise stated, California law compels cars to restrict their speed to 25 mph when traveling through residential areas. This is done to protect the wellbeing of nearby motorists, bikers, and pedestrians.

2. What should you do if a bicycle is coming at you from the opposite direction while you are driving?
Answer: When passing a biker, you should allow them at least 3 feet of space and be mindful of their actions and any possible dangers.

Explanation: On the road, bikers have the same rights and obligations as drivers. When passing them, drivers should leave at least 3 feet between vehicles and be mindful of their movements and any possible dangers, such as unexpected stops or twists.

3. When is it acceptable to use a phone while operating a vehicle?
Answer: Only if your phone has a hands-free feature are you allowed to use it while driving.
Explanation: Using a portable phone while driving is against California law. However, if a mobile phone has a hands-free gadget, such a Bluetooth earpiece, it is acceptable to use it.

4. What should you do if you're driving and a pedestrian is using a clearly designated crosswalk to cross the street?
Answer: In order to prevent an accident, you should give the pedestrian the right of way and drive carefully.
Explanation: When crossing at a designated crosswalk, pedestrians especially have the right of way on the road. In order to avoid an accident, drivers should yield to pedestrians and drive carefully.

5. On a two-lane road, what should you do if a bike is traveling in the same direction as you?
Answer: When passing a biker, you should leave at least 3 feet between you and them and should only do so when it's safe to do so.
Explanation: Drivers should offer bicycles at least 3 feet of space while passing them if they want to utilize the road. Drivers must be cautious and pass cyclists only when it is safe to do so.

6. When should a driver turn on their warning lights?
Answer: while your car is disabled or stopped on the road, or while you're participating in a funeral procession, you should turn on your hazard lights.

Explanation: When a car is stopped or disabled on the road, or when it is part of a funeral procession, hazard lights are used to signal this. Using danger lights while driving in regular traffic is not recommended.

7. What should you do if a bike is coming at you from behind while you're driving?
Answer: You should keep your pace and position in the lane and let the bicycle past when it's safe to do so.
Explanation: When sharing the road in a bike lane or on a small route, bicycles may come up behind automobiles. When it is safe to do so, drivers should maintain their speed and position in the lane while providing the biker at least 3 feet of space as they pass. Additionally, motorists should exercise caution when turning or changing lanes since a bicycle may be in their blind area.

8. What should you do if a person is crossing the street while you're driving and they're facing oncoming traffic?
Answer: In order to prevent an accident, you should give the pedestrian the right of way and drive carefully.
Explanation: Even though a pedestrian is facing vehicles when crossing a street, they still have the right of way. In order to avoid an accident, drivers should yield to pedestrians and drive carefully.

9. What should you do if a bike is using the right side of the lane while you are driving?
Answer: You should give the bicycle at least 3 feet of space and only pass them when it is safe to do so.
Explanation: Bicyclists are allowed to use the road and may ride in the right-hand lane. Only when it is safe should drivers overtake cyclists, giving them at least 3 feet of clearance.

10. What should you do if a pedestrian is attempting to cross the

road at an unmarked crosswalk while you are driving?
Answer: In order to prevent an accident, you should give the pedestrian the right of way and drive carefully.
Explanation: Even if they are crossing at an unmarked crosswalk, pedestrians have the right of way on the road. In order to avoid an accident, drivers should yield to pedestrians and drive carefully.

Alcohol and drug awareness

1. What are the legal repercussions of driving while impaired by prescription medication in California?
Answer: Driving while impaired by prescription medication is prohibited in the state of California and carries the same penalties as driving while intoxicated by alcohol.
Explanation: Driving under the influence of prescription medicines is prohibited in California and carries the same fines, license suspension, and potential jail time as driving under the influence of alcohol.

2. What happens when various substances or alcohol are combined?
Answer: Mixing multiple substances might raise the likelihood of adverse effects and make it more difficult for a driver to drive safely.
Explanation: Mixing multiple substances might raise the chance of negative side effects and make it more difficult for someone to drive safely. Understanding the possible consequences of various drugs will help you avoid drinking them together.

3. What should you do if you are impaired by alcohol or drugs and are driving?
Answer: You should stop in a secure area and wait until the symptoms subside, or find another transportation.
Explanation: If you are driving and you start to feel the affects of alcohol or drugs, stop right away and move to a safe place. You should also make arrangements for alternate

transportation until the symptoms subside.

4. What are the legal repercussions of refusing to undergo a field sobriety test after being stopped by the police?
Answer: Penalties like license suspension or revocation may occur from refusing to perform a field sobriety test.
Explanation: When stopped by law enforcement, refusing to complete a field sobriety test might result in fines, license suspension or revocation, as well as other legal repercussions.

5. What does California's "zero tolerance" statute entail?
Answer: Under the "zero tolerance" regulation, drivers under the age of 21 may be subject to fines for having any level of alcohol in their systems.
Explanation: Under California law, drivers under 21 may be fined for having any level of alcohol in their systems. This is known as the "zero tolerance" statute. This is within the 0.08% legal blood alcohol limit for drivers who are at least 21 years old.

6. How does drug or alcohol use affect one's capacity for risk perception?
Answer: Using drugs or alcohol might make it more difficult for someone to see risks and make wise choices.
Explanation: Using drugs or alcohol can decrease a person's capacity for risk perception and responsible decision-making, increasing the likelihood of accidents or other risky circumstances.

7. What are the legal repercussions of driving while under the influence of alcohol and drugs?
Answer: It's against the law to drive in California while under the influence of both drugs and alcohol. Penalties for this offense are the same as for driving while under the influence of just one of them.
Explanation: Driving while under the influence of both alcohol and drugs is

prohibited in California and carries the same fines, license suspension, and potential jail time as driving while under the influence of just one of the substances.

8. What should you do if one of your party guests becomes inebriated while you are hosting?
Answer: You should make sure the visitor isn't driving, and you might need to make arrangements for alternate transportation or let the visitor stay over.
Explanation: You are in charge of ensuring that your visitors are safe as the party host. If one of your visitors becomes drunk, you should make sure they don't drive, and you might need to get them a ride somewhere else or let them stay the night.

9. In California, what are the legal repercussions of using over-the-counter drugs while driving?
Answer: Driving while under the influence of over-the-counter pharmaceuticals is prohibited in California and carries the same penalties as driving while impaired by prescription medication or alcohol.
Explanation: Driving under the influence of over-the-counter pharmaceuticals is prohibited in California and carries the same fines, license suspension, and potential jail time as driving under the influence of alcohol or prescription drugs.

10. How does drug or alcohol use affect a person's capacity to respond to unforeseen circumstances on the road?
Answer: Using drugs or alcohol can make it harder for a person to react to unforeseen circumstances on the road, which increases the likelihood of accidents or other risky scenarios.
Explanation: Using drugs or alcohol can make it difficult for a person to react appropriately to unforeseen circumstances on the road, increasing the likelihood of accidents or other risky scenarios.

Vehicle operation and maintenance

1. What does an automobile's air conditioning system serve?
Answer: To make driving more pleasant and secure, a car's air conditioning system cools and dehumidifies the air within.
Explanation: In hot and muggy weather, a car's air conditioning system is intended to chill and dehumidify the air within the vehicle, assisting in lowering driver fatigue and enhancing visibility.

2. How frequently should a gasoline filter be changed in a car?
Answer: Depending on the make and model of the vehicle, the suggested mileage ranges from 20,000 to 40,000 miles for gasoline filter replacement.
Explanation: Depending on the make and model of the vehicle, the suggested time between gasoline filter replacements varies, but is normally between 20,000 and 40,000 miles, or every two to four years.

3. What does a car's power steering system serve?
Answer: A car's power steering system helps the driver navigate the automobile more easily and with more control.
Explanation: A car's power steering system helps the driver steer the automobile by making it easier to spin the wheels and enhancing control and maneuverability.

4. How frequently should you change your car's gearbox fluid?
Answer: Depending on the make and model of the vehicle, the recommended interval for refilling the transmission fluid varies from 3 0 0 to 6 0 0 miles.
Explanation: Depending on the make and type of the vehicle, the recommended time between transmission fluid replacements ranges from 30,000 to 60,000 miles, or every two to four years.

5. What does a catalytic converter do in a car?
Answer: The catalytic converter in a car's engine reduces hazardous emissions and transforms them into less dangerous gases before they are discharged into the atmosphere.
Explanation: To enhance air quality and lower pollution, a car's catalytic converter is made to minimize harmful emissions from the engine and transform them into less dangerous gases before they are discharged into the environment.

6. How frequently should windshield wipers on an automobile be replaced?
Answer: Depending on the make and model of the vehicle, the recommended time for changing windshield wipers varies from six months to a year.
Explanation: Depending on the make and model of the vehicle, the suggested frequency for changing the windshield wipers is different, but generally speaking, it falls between six months and a year, or whenever they start to show indications of wear and tear.

7. What does a car's differential serve?
Answer: The differential on a car's wheels distributes power between them and enables them to rotate at various speeds during turns, improving handling and stability.
Explanation: Especially in cars with rear-wheel or all-wheel drive, the differential of an automobile is intended to transfer power between the wheels and allow them to rotate at various speeds during turns, improving handling and stability.

8. How frequently should a car's serpentine belt be changed?
Answer: Depending on the make and model of the automobile, the suggested time for serpentine belt replacement varies, but it normally falls between 60,000 and 100,000 miles.
Explanation: Depending on the make and type of the vehicle, a serpentine belt replacement is normally advised every 60,000 to 100,000 miles, or every five to seven years.

9. What does a car's throttle body serve?
Answer: The throttle body of an automobile is designed to control the amount of air that enters the engine, hence regulating engine speed and power.
Explanation: A car's throttle body is made to control the amount of air that enters the engine, hence regulating the engine's speed and power output and assisting in achieving the best performance and fuel economy possible.

10. How often should the engine air filter be changed in a car?
Answer: The suggested time for replacing a car's engine air filter varies based on the make and model of the vehicle, but generally speaking, it's between 1 and 5 miles (or 1 to 0).
Explanation: Depending on the make and type of the vehicle, the suggested time between engine air filter replacements varies, but often falls between 15,000 and 30,000 miles, or every year or two.

Emergency situations and procedures
1. What should you do if your car's engine overheats while you're driving?
Answer: If you are driving and the engine of your car overheats, you should pull over at a safe place, turn off the engine, and wait for it to cool down before you check the coolant level.
Explanation: If the engine of your car overheats, it might harm the engine and make collisions more likely. Pull over to a secure area, turn off the engine, and wait for it to cool before examining the coolant level to reduce the possibility of further damage.

2. What should you do if your car's accelerator pedal becomes stuck while you're driving?

Answer: If you're driving and the accelerator pedal on your car becomes stuck, you should put the car in neutral, guide it to a safe place, and then come to a complete stop.
Explanation: If the accelerator pedal of your car gets stuck, the car could accelerate suddenly. Put the car in neutral to disconnect the motor from the wheels, navigate to a safe area, then stop the car to restore control.

3. What should you do if the battery warning light on your car illuminates while you are driving?
Answer: If the battery warning light on your car comes on while you're driving, you should switch off any unneeded electrical equipment, such the radio or air conditioning, and head to a repair facility or service station so the battery and charging system may be inspected.
Explanation: If the battery warning light on your car illuminates, there can be an issue with the battery or charging system. Turn off any superfluous electrical equipment to reduce the likelihood of a failure, then drive to a repair facility or service station to have the battery and charging system inspected.

4. What should you do if your car's brakes fail while you're driving?
Answer: If your car's brakes fail while you're driving, you should shift down to a lower gear, apply the parking brake, and maneuver the car to a safe spot to stop.
Explanation: It may be challenging to stop or slow down your car if its brakes fail. Downshift into a lower gear, activate the parking brake to slow down the car, then steer to a safe place to stop it to reduce the likelihood of a collision.

5. What should you do if your car's gearbox breaks down while you are driving?
Answer: If your car's transmission breaks down while you're driving, stop in a safe spot, turn off the engine, and dial for a tow truck.

Explanation: If the transmission in your car breaks down, the car may lose power and become challenging to drive. Pull over to a safe area, turn off the engine, and dial for a tow truck to reduce the chance of an accident.

6. What should you do if your car's airbag deploys while you are driving?
Answer: If your airbag deploys while you are driving, you should stop the car, turn off the engine, and look inside for any wounds.
Explanation: When the airbag in your car deploys, there may be a loud roar and a shocking jolt. Stop the car, switch off the engine, and look around for any injuries to make sure you and any passengers are safe.

7. What should you do if you notice that your car's engine is overheating while you are driving?
Answer: If you are driving and the temperature gauge on your car indicates that the engine is overheating, you should pull over to a safe place, switch off the engine, and wait for it to cool down before checking the coolant level.
Explanation: If the temperature gauge on your car indicates that the engine is overheating, this might harm the engine and raise the possibility of an accident. Pull over to a secure area, turn off the engine, and wait for it to cool before examining the coolant level to reduce the possibility of further damage.

8. What should you do if the oil pressure warning light on your car illuminates while you are driving?
Answer: If you are driving and your vehicle's oil pressure warning light comes on, you should pull over to a safe location, turn off the engine, and check the oil level.
Explanation: If the oil pressure warning light on your car illuminates, it may be a sign that there is a problem with the oil pressure or oil level. Check the oil level, pull over to a safe area, and turn off the engine to

reduce the possibility of engine damage.

9. What should you do if your car's power steering breaks while you're driving?
Answer: If your car's power steering fails while you're driving, stop in a safe spot, turn off the engine, and check the fluid level.
Explanation: If your car's power steering malfunctions, driving may become challenging. Pull over to a safe area, turn off the engine, and check the power steering fluid level to reduce the likelihood of a crash.

10. What should you do if a tire blows out while you are driving?
Answer: If a tire blows out while you are driving, maintain your hands on the wheel, gradually reduce your speed, and navigate to a safe spot to change the tire.
Explanation: If a tire blows out while you're driving, the car could pull to one side or becoming unstable. Keep your hands on the wheel, gradually slow down, and drive the car to a safe spot to change the tire if you want to keep it under control.

Practice Test 4:
Traffic laws, Driving rules and regulations
1. In California, how far should you keep a gap from a bike when passing?
Answer: At least 3 feet
Explanation: When passing a bike in California, you must keep at least a 3-foot separation.

2. What should you do if you are driving down a street in California and you come across a person who is attempting to cross the roadway at an unmarked intersection?
Answer: Give the pedestrian the right-of-way and, if necessary, completely stop.
Explanation: If you're driving on a roadway in California and you notice a pedestrian crossing the street at an unsignalized junction, you must yield to the pedestrian and, if necessary, come to a complete stop.

3. What is the top speed limit for cars traveling on a two-lane, undivided California highway?
Answer: 55 miles per hour
Explanation: Unless otherwise indicated, the top speed limit for cars traveling on a two-lane undivided roadway in California is 55 miles per hour.

4. What should you do if you come into thick fog while traveling along a California highway?
Answer: Reduce your speed, activate your low-beam headlights, and get ready to stop.
Explanation: If you're traveling in deep fog on a California roadway, you should slow down, activate your low-beam headlights, and be ready to stop.

5. How fast are cars allowed to go on a Californian street in a business district?
Answer: 25 miles per hour
Explanation: Unless otherwise marked, the top speed restriction for cars traveling along a street in a business area in California is 25 miles per hour.

6. What should you do if you come across a cyclist in a bicycle lane in California?
Answer: Avoid using the cycling lane when driving, and give way to cyclists.
Explanation: If you come across a cyclist in a bicycle lane in California, you must not drive in the lane and give the cyclist the right-of-way.

7. What is the top speed limit for cars traveling down a residential street in California?
Answer: 25 miles per hour
Explanation: Unless otherwise marked, the top speed restriction for cars traveling along a street in a residential area of California is 25 miles per hour.

8. What should you do if you encounter a sign warning of impending road maintenance while travelling on a Californian highway?
Answer: Drive more slowly, be ready to stop, and obey all construction personnel's directions.
Explanation: If you notice a sign warning that there will be road work ahead while traveling on a California highway, you should slow down, be ready to stop, and obey whatever directions the construction workers may give you.

9. How fast are cars allowed to go on a Californian street in front of a school when kids are playing outside or crossing the street?
Answer: 25 miles per hour
Explanation: Unless otherwise marked, the maximum speed restriction for cars traveling on a California roadway near a school when kids are playing outdoors or crossing the street is 25 miles per hour.

10. What should you do if you encounter a sign warning of a bend while travelling on a Californian highway?
Answer: Be ready to change your speed and steering as needed by slowing down before the bend.
Explanation: If you are driving on a California highway and you notice a sign warning you that there is a curve ahead, you should slow down and be ready to alter your speed and steering as needed.

Road signs and signals
1. What does a rectangular sign with a green bicycle emblem and black words or symbols on a white backdrop mean?
Answer: It indicates a designated bike lane.
Explanation: A rectangular sign designating a dedicated bike lane has a white backdrop, black wording or symbols, and a green bicycle emblem. When cycling on the road, bikers should ride in this lane.

2. What does a rectangular sign that reads "yield ahead" and has a red border and a white backdrop mean?
Answer: It indicates that a yield sign is ahead.
Explanation: Drivers should be ready to yield to incoming vehicles or pedestrians when they see a rectangular sign with the words "yield ahead" on a white background and red border.

3. What does a circular sign that reads "do not enter" and has a red border and a white backdrop mean?
Answer: It means that vehicles are not permitted to enter the road or go in the same direction.
Explanation: Drivers aren't permitted to enter the road or the direction of movement, as indicated by a circular sign with the words "do not enter" on it with a white backdrop and red border. Drivers need to find another route.

4. What does a rectangular sign that says "no U-turn" and has a red circle and slash across it indicate? It has a white backdrop and black wording or symbols.
Answer: It says that at the junction, U-turns are not allowed.
Explanation: A rectangular sign with black lettering or symbols on a white background, a red circle and slash through it, and the words "no U-turn" denote that turning left or right at the intersection is not permitted. A different route must be found by drivers.

5. What does a rectangular sign with "no pedestrians" written in red letters with a red circle and slash across it with a white backdrop and black wording or symbols denote?
Answer: It says that people walking on the sidewalk are not permitted.
Explanation: A rectangular sign with a white backdrop, black letters or symbols, a red circle, a slash across it, and the phrase "no pedestrians" denotes that pedestrians are not permitted on the road. Alternative routes must be found by pedestrians.

6. What does a rectangular sign that reads "speed limit" and has a yellow diamond symbol in the center and black letters or symbols on a white backdrop mean?
Answer: It indicates the maximum speed limit allowed on the roadway.
Explanation: The maximum speed restriction on the road is indicated by a rectangular sign with a white background and black letters or symbols, a yellow diamond symbol in the middle, and the words "speed limit." The prescribed speed restriction must be followed by drivers.

7. What does a rectangular sign with a green circle and the words "go" or an arrow pointing to the right, with a black backdrop and letters or symbols, indicate?
Answer: It designates a lane that can be used for turning right or moving forward.
Explanation: A rectangular sign with a white backdrop and black wording or symbols, together with a green circle and the words "go" or an arrow pointing to the right, designates a lane for turning right or moving forward straight ahead.

8. What does a rectangular sign that reads "school zone" and has a red border and a white backdrop mean?
Answer: It indicates a school zone where children may be present.
Explanation: A school zone is one where children may be present, as indicated by a rectangular sign with the words "school zone" written on it and a red border around it. Drivers ought to reduce their speed and be ready to stop if required.

9. What does a rectangular sign with the words "handicapped parking only" and a blue circle with a white backdrop and black letters or symbols mean?
Answer: It denotes a parking area set aside for people with impairments.
Explanation: A rectangular sign with a blue circle and the words "handicapped parking only," on a white background, is used to identify a parking area for people with impairments. This area is only available for use by cars with a current disability parking placard or license plate.

10. What does a rectangular sign with "no honking" written in red with a red circle and slash across it on a white backdrop and black letters or symbols denote?
Answer: It says that it's not allowed to sound the horn in that region.
Explanation: A rectangular sign with a white backdrop and black letters or symbols, a red circle and slash across it, and the phrase "no honking," denotes that blaring the horn is forbidden in the area and that offenders may face fines or penalties.

Safe driving practices, pedestrians, and bicyclists
1. What should you do if a pedestrian is walking on the sidewalk in the same direction as you while you are driving?
Answer: If the pedestrian is walking close to the road, you should drive carefully and pay attention to their actions.
Explanation: Drivers should be alert to pedestrians' actions on sidewalks since they have the right of way, especially if they are crossing the street. Additionally, drivers need to exercise caution while turning or entering/exiting driveways since they can be blindsided by a pedestrian.

2. When is parking in a bike lane acceptable?
Answer: Parking in a bike lane is never permitted.
Explanation: Parking in a bike lane might endanger other automobiles as well as bicycles because bike lanes are only intended for use by cyclists. In a bike lane, parking is never permitted.

3. What should you do if you're driving and a pedestrian is using a

crosswalk but there isn't a traffic light at the crosswalk?
Answer: Passing other cars that have stopped for a pedestrian is not appropriate; you should give them the right of way.
Explanation: Even though a crosswalk lacks a traffic light, pedestrians still have the right-of-way in certain areas. When passing another vehicle that has stopped for a pedestrian, drivers should yield to the pedestrian and not try to overtake them.

4. What should you do if a bicycle is riding in a bike lane to your right while you are driving?
Answer: To prevent cutting off the bicycle, check your blind spots and mirrors before making a right turn.
Explanation: Motorists should be alert to cyclists' movements to prevent collisions. Bicyclists have the right to utilize bike lanes. Drivers should make sure there are no bicycles in their route by checking their mirrors and blind zones before making a right turn.

5. What should you do if a person is crossing the street against the flow of traffic while you are driving?
Answer: In order to prevent an accident, you should give the pedestrian the right of way and drive carefully.
Explanation: Even while walking against the flow of traffic, pedestrians have the right of way on the road. In order to avoid an accident, drivers should yield to pedestrians and drive carefully.

6. What should you do if a bunch of cyclists is passing you while you're driving?
Answer: You should allow the bicycles more room and be mindful of their actions and any possible dangers, including unexpected stops or twists.
Explanation: Drivers should allow additional room for bicycles and be alert to their movements and any risks. Bicyclists may ride in groups. Drivers should exercise caution while

passing a group of bikers and refrain from passing if it is unsafe to do so.

7. What should you do if a pedestrian is using headphones and crossing the street while you're driving?
Answer: You should yield the right of way to the pedestrian and exercise caution to avoid a collision, as the pedestrian may not be able to hear your vehicle approaching.
Explanation: Even if they are using headphones and may not be able to hear your car approaching, pedestrians have the right of way on the road. In order to avoid an accident, drivers should yield to pedestrians and drive carefully.

8. What should you do if a bicycle is riding in a bike lane to your left while you are driving?
Answer: You should be mindful of the bicyclist's actions and any possible dangers, and you should only attempt to pass them when it is safe to do so.
Explanation: Drivers should be alert to the movements and possible dangers of bicyclists riding in the bike lanes to the left of the road. Unless it is safe to do so, drivers should take caution and avoid attempting to pass cyclists.

9. What action should you take if you are driving and a pedestrian is using a phone to text while walking on the road?
Answer: Since the pedestrian might not be aware of their surroundings, you should yield to them and drive carefully to avoid an accident.
Explanation: Even though they are inattentive and may not be aware of their surroundings, pedestrians have the right of way on the road. In order to avoid an accident, drivers should yield to pedestrians and drive carefully.

10. What should you do if you're driving down a one-way street and a bicycle is cycling in the same direction as you?
Answer: When passing a biker, you should leave at least 3 feet between

you and them and should only do so when it's safe to do so.
Explanation: Drivers should offer bicycles at least 3 feet of space while passing them if they want to utilize the road.

Alcohol and drug awareness
1. In California, what is the legal blood alcohol content (BAC) limit for commercial drivers?
Answer: In California, 0.04% is the legal blood alcohol content (BAC) limit for commercial drivers.
Explanation: Commercial drivers in California are subject to a tougher standard, with a permissible BAC limit of 0. 0 4 percent, which is half the maximum for non-commercial drivers.

2. In California, what are the legal repercussions of driving while high on methamphetamine?
Answer: Driving while impaired by methamphetamine is banned in California and carries the same penalties as driving while impaired by other drugs or alcohol.
Explanation: Driving under the influence of methamphetamine is prohibited in California and carries the same fines, license suspension, and potential jail time as driving under the influence of other narcotics or alcohol.

3. How does long-term drug or alcohol use affect a person's ability to drive?
Answer: Even when a person is not actively under the influence of drugs or alcohol, long-term use can damage their ability to drive.
Explanation: It's crucial to avoid taking drugs or alcohol while driving since they can cause lasting brain changes and damage a person's ability to drive even when they are not actively intoxicated.

4. In California, what are the legal repercussions of giving alcohol to a minor?
Answer: It's against the law to give alcohol to a child in California, and

doing so may result in fines, community service, and other sanctions.
Explanation: It is unlawful to give alcohol to a juvenile in California, and violators may be subject to fines, community service requirements, and other sanctions even if they are not the youngster's parents or legal guardians.

5. In California, what are the legal repercussions of inhalant-impaired driving?
Answer: Driving while impaired by inhalants is prohibited in California and carries the same penalties as driving while impaired by other drugs or alcohol.
Explanation: Driving while intoxicated by inhalants is prohibited in California and carries the same fines, license suspension, and potential jail time as driving while under the influence of other drugs or alcohol.

6. How does weariness affect a person's ability to drive?
Answer: Fatigue can make it difficult for someone to drive by reducing concentration and awareness and lowering response time.
Explanation: It's critical to obtain enough rest before operating a vehicle since fatigue can affect a person's ability to drive by reducing response time and lowering concentration and awareness.

7. What should you do if you believe a person you know is operating a vehicle while under the influence of alcohol or drugs?
Answer: You should urge the individual to find other transportation or offer to drive them personally. If required, you should also notify legal authorities.
Explanation: If you have reason to believe that a friend or family member is operating a vehicle while under the influence of alcohol or drugs, you should urge them to find other transportation or offer to drive them yourself. You may need to ask

the police for help if they refuse or are unable to do so.

8. In California, what are the legal repercussions of using hallucinogens while driving?
Answer: Driving while high on hallucinogens is prohibited in California and carries the same penalties as driving when intoxicated by other drugs or alcohol.
Explanation: Driving while under the influence of hallucinogens is prohibited in California and carries the same fines, license suspension, and potential jail time as driving while under the influence of other drugs or alcohol.

9. How can stress or anxiety affect a person's ability to drive?
Answer: Stress or anxiety can make it difficult for a person to drive safely since it causes distractions and slows down attention and reflexes.
Explanation: It's crucial to deal with stress and anxiety before driving since they can hinder a person's ability to focus, respond quickly, and increase distraction.

10. In California, what are the legal repercussions of operating a vehicle when your license is suspended or revoked?
Answer: It's against the law to drive in California with a license that has been suspended or revoked, and doing so can result in fines, jail time, and an extension of the suspension or revocation term.
Explanation: It's against the law to drive in California if your license is suspended or revoked. You might face fines, jail time, and an extension of the suspension or revocation term.

Vehicle operation and maintenance
1. What does a car's brake fluid serve?
Answer: Brake fluid in a car's brakes transmits pressure from the brake pedal to the brakes, enabling the automobile to slow down and stop.

Explanation: Brake fluid, a hydraulic liquid, sends pressure from the brake pedal to the braking system, enabling the car to slow down and stop. It serves as a crucial part of the braking system.

2. How frequently should the engine oil be changed in a car?
Answer: Depending on the make and model of the automobile, the recommended oil change interval varies from 5 to 7 miles.
Explanation: Depending on the make and type of the vehicle, the recommended time between engine oil changes ranges from 5,000 to 7,500 miles, or every six months to a year.

3. What function does a car's suspension system serve?
Answer: A car's suspension system's job is to keep the tires in touch with the road surface while also absorbing shocks and vibrations from the road to give the ride a smooth and comfortable feel.
Explanation: A car's suspension system is made to keep the tires in touch with the road surface, which is crucial for safety and handling, while also absorbing shocks and vibrations from the road to provide a smooth and comfortable ride.

4. How frequently should an automobile's engine coolant be changed?
Answer: Depending on the make and model of the vehicle, the recommended interval for replenishing the engine coolant varies from 3 to 0 to 5 miles.
Explanation: Depending on the make and type of the vehicle, the recommended time between engine coolant replacements ranges from 30,000 to 50,000 miles, or every two to three years.

5. What does an air filter in an automobile do?
Answer: The air filter's job is to filter out debris like dirt and dust from the air that enters the engine, preventing

harm and ensuring peak performance.
Explanation: To prevent damage to the engine and to maintain peak performance, the air filter in an automobile is made to filter out dust, grime, and other impurities from the air that enters the engine.

6. How frequently should you check the tire pressure on your car?
Answer: At least once per month is the suggested frequency for monitoring a car's tire pressure.
Explanation: Regular tire pressure checks are necessary to make sure a car's tires are properly inflated, which enhances handling, safety, and fuel economy.

7. What function does a car's powertrain serve?
Answer: A car's powertrain is responsible for transferring power from the engine to the wheels, which enables the automobile to move.
Explanation: A car's powertrain is the mechanism that sends energy from the engine to the wheels, enabling the car to drive. It consists of the driveshaft, differential, and gearbox.

8. How frequently should a car's cabin air filter be changed?
Answer 0: The suggested period for replacing a car's cabin air filter varies based on the make and model of the vehicle, but generally speaking, it's between 12,000 and 15,000 miles, or 12,000 to 20,000 miles.
Explanation: A car's cabin air filter is made to take pollutants like pollen, dust, and other irritants out of the air that enters the cabin. Depending on the make and type of the vehicle, the suggested replacement time might range from 12,000 to 15,000 kilometers, or every year or two.

9. What does windshield washer fluid do for a car?
Answer: The windshield washer fluid in a car is designed to clean the windshield and increase visibility while driving.

Explanation: To clean out dirt, dust, and other particles from the windshield, windshield washer fluid is a specifically prepared liquid that is sprayed onto the glass. It is crucial for safe driving since it aids in maintaining visibility.

10. How frequently should brake fluid be changed in a car?
Answer: Depending on the make and model of the vehicle, the recommended brake fluid replacement period normally falls between 24,000 and 36,000 miles.
Explanation: Brake fluid, a hydraulic fluid, is susceptible to absorbing moisture and being contaminated over time. This can have an impact on how well the braking system works. Depending on the make and type of the vehicle, the suggested replacement frequency normally runs from 24,000 to 36,000 miles, or every two to three years.

Emergency situations and procedures
1. What should you do if your car's headlights fail while you're driving?
Answer: Use your warning lights and pull over to a safe place if you are driving and your car's headlights go out.
Explanation: If your car's headlights fail, it may be harder for other drivers to see you and lessen your visibility. Use your warning lights to warn other cars and stop in a safe area to reduce the likelihood of a collision.

2. What should you do if your car's windshield wipers fail to operate in a downpour while you are driving?
Answer: If you're driving and the windshield wipers on your car stop functioning in a downpour, you should pull over to a safe place and wait for the rain to cease, or you may use a cloth to wipe the windshield manually.
Explanation: If your car's windshield wipers fail to function in a downpour, it might make it harder to see and raise the possibility of a crash. Pull over to a safe area and wait for the rain to stop, or physically wipe the

windshield with a towel, to reduce the chance of a crash.

3. What should you do if your car's gas pedal becomes stuck while you're driving?
Answer: If you're driving and your car's gas pedal becomes stuck, you should put the car in neutral, navigate to a safe place, and then come to a complete stop.
Explanation: If the gas pedal on your car gets stuck, the car could accelerate violently. Put the car in neutral to disconnect the motor from the wheels, navigate to a safe area, then stop the car to restore control.

4. What should you do if your car's steering wheel locks up while you're driving it?
Answer: If your car's steering wheel locks up while you're driving, you should try to unlock it by twisting the key in the ignition or depressing the brake pedal, then steer to a safe place to stop the car.
Explanation: If the steering wheel in your car locks up, it might be challenging to maintain control of the vehicle. Try to unlock the lock by twisting the key in the ignition or depressing the brake pedal to recover control of the car, then drive it to a safe spot to come to a halt.

5. What should you do if your car's brake pedal feels mushy or drops to the floor while you're driving?
Answer: If you are driving and the brake pedal on your car feels spongy or goes all the way to the floor, you should gently pump the brakes, downshift, and maneuver to a safe place to stop the car.
Explanation: If the brake pedal in your car feels spongy or travels all the way to the floor, there could be an issue with the braking system. Pump the brakes softly, downshift into a lower gear, and direct the car to a safe stop spot to reduce the chance of an accident.

6. What should you do if the check engine light on your car illuminates while you are driving?
Answer: You should take your car to a garage or gas station to get it serviced if the check engine light on your car illuminates while you are driving.
Explanation: If the check engine light on your car illuminates, it can mean there's an issue with the emissions system or engine. Drive to a repair facility or gas station to get the car inspected in order to reduce the likelihood of a breakdown.

7. What should you do if your car's air conditioner stops working when you're traveling on a hot day?
Answer: On a hot day, if you're driving and the air conditioning in your car breaks down, you should roll down the windows and stop in a safe spot to cool down before continuing.
Explanation: When your car's air conditioning breaks down on a hot day, it can be uncomfortable and distracting. Roll down the windows and stop in a secure area to cool off before continuing to drive to reduce the danger of an accident.

8. What should you do if, while driving, your car's warning lights suddenly begin to flash?
Answer: If you are driving and suddenly notice that your danger lights are flashing, you should stop in a safe place and turn them off.
Explanation: It might be confusing and distracting for other drivers if your car's danger lights suddenly start flashing while you're driving. Pull over to a safe area, switch off your warning lights, and reduce the chance of an accident.

9. What should you do if your car's exhaust system suddenly starts generating loud noises while you're driving?
Answer: You should take your car to a repair facility or service station to have the exhaust system examined if it starts producing loud noises while you're driving.

Explanation: If the exhaust system in your car starts generating loud noises, there can be an issue with the muffler or exhaust system. Drive to a repair facility or gas station to get it inspected in order to reduce the possibility of a breakdown or additional damage.

10. What should you do if a sudden loss of electricity occurs while you are driving?
Answer: If you suddenly lose power while driving, you should try to relocate your car safely to the side of the road and switch on your warning lights.
Explanation: While driving, a sudden lack of power might make it challenging to keep control of your car and raise the possibility of an accident. Try to carefully relocate your car to the side of the road and activate your warning lights to warn other vehicles in order to reduce the likelihood of a collision. After stopping, you may evaluate the problem and take the necessary action, such dialing for roadside help or inspecting the car's engine.

Practice Test 5:
Traffic laws, Driving rules and regulations
1. How fast are cars allowed to go down an alleyway on a California street?
Answer: 15 miles per hour
Explanation: In an alley on a California street, a car is only allowed to travel at a maximum speed of 15 miles per hour.

2. What should you do if you observe a blind person with a white cane or a guide dog while driving along a California street?
Answer: Reverse your direction and give the pedestrian the right-of-way.
Explanation: If you are driving in California and you encounter a blind person walking with a white cane or a guide dog, you must stop your car and give the person the right-of-way.

3. In a school zone, what is the top speed restriction for cars traveling down a Californian street?
Answer: 25 miles per hour
Explanation: Unless otherwise indicated, the top speed restriction for cars traveling through a school zone in California is 25 miles per hour.

4. What should you do if you notice a sign signaling a halt ahead while traveling on a California highway?
Answer: Reduce your speed and get ready to stop completely when you see a stop sign or signal.
Explanation: If you are driving in California and you notice a sign warning you that there will be a stop ahead, you should slow down and be ready to stop completely at the stop sign or signal.

5. On a California highway, what is the top speed limit for cars pulling a home trailer?
Answer: 55 miles per hour
Explanation: Unless otherwise indicated, the top speed restriction for cars pulling a house trailer on a California roadway is 55 mph.

6. What should you do if you're driving down a street in California and you notice a pedestrian crossing the roadway with a "DON'T WALK" or "RAISED HAND" sign blinking in front of them?
Answer: Stay out of the crosswalk and give the pedestrian the right-of-way.
Explanation: If you are driving on a California roadway and you notice a pedestrian crossing the street with a flashing "DON'T WALK" or "RAISED HAND" signal, you must give the right of way to the pedestrian and refrain from crossing the street yourself.

7. In a senior center zone on a Californian roadway, what is the top speed restriction for moving vehicles?
Answer: 15 miles per hour
Explanation: In a senior center zone on a California street, the top speed

restriction for moving cars is 15 miles per hour.

8. What should you do if you are driving down a roadway in California and you come across a person using the crosswalk when the "WALK" signal is steady?
Answer: Stay out of the crosswalk and give the pedestrian the right-of-way.
Explanation: If you are driving on a California roadway and you notice a pedestrian crossing the street with a steady "WALK" signal, you must defer to the person and refrain from crossing yourself.

9. How fast are cars allowed to go on a Californian street in a business district?
Answer: 25 miles per hour
Explanation: Unless otherwise marked, the top speed restriction for cars traveling along a street in a business area in California is 25 miles per hour.

10. What should you do if you encounter a sign warning of an impending diversion while travelling on a Californian highway?
Answer: Go slowly and adhere to the construction workers' directions and diversion signs.
Explanation: If you observe a sign warning of an impending detour while traveling on a Californian highway, you should slow down and obey the detour signs and instructions provided by construction personnel.

Road signs and signals
1. What does a rectangular sign with "no bicycles" written in red letters with a red circle and slash across it with a white backdrop and black wording or symbols denote?
Answer: It means that bicycles are not permitted on the road.
Explanation: Bicycles are not permitted on the street, as indicated by a rectangular sign with a white background and black letters or symbols, a red circle, a slash across

it, and the words "no bicycles." Riders on bicycles must find another path.

2. What does a rectangular sign that reads "guide sign" and has a white backdrop and green text mean?
Answer: It denotes a sign that offers instructions or background data on a location.
Explanation: A rectangular sign with the words "guide sign" written in green letters on a white backdrop designates a sign that offers directions or information about a location. Usually, important roads and highways have these signs.

3. What does a circular sign that reads "stop" and has a red border and white lettering mean?
Answer: It means that vehicles must stop entirely before moving forward.
Explanation: Drivers must completely stop before moving on, according to a circular sign with the words "stop" on it with a white backdrop and red border. When approaching a crosswalk or white stop line, drivers must stop, yield to pedestrians, and then proceed.

4. What does a rectangular sign with the words "construction zone" and a yellow diamond symbol in the middle, black letters or symbols on a white backdrop, denote?
Answer: It warns of a construction area up ahead where there may be employees.
Explanation: A rectangular sign with a white backdrop and black letters or symbols, a yellow diamond symbol in the middle, and the words "construction zone," denotes a construction zone up ahead where workers could be present. Drivers need to slow down and be ready for lane closures and detours.

5. What does a rectangular sign that says "no left turn" and has a red circle and slash across it indicate? The sign has a white backdrop and black wording or symbols.
Answer: It means that the crossing forbids left turns.

Explanation: A rectangular sign with black letters or symbols, a red circle and slash across it, and the phrase "no left turn" denotes that left turns are forbidden at the intersection. Drivers need to find a another route.

6. What does a rectangular sign with a green circle and the words "bicycle route" in black letters or symbols on a white backdrop mean?
Answer: It indicates a designated route for bicycles.
Explanation: A rectangular sign with a green circle and the words "bicycle route," together with a white backdrop and black letters or symbols, designates a route for bicycles. If cycling on a road, riders should choose this path.

7. What does a rectangular sign with "no parking" written in red with a red circle and slash across it on a white backdrop and black letters or symbols denote?
Answer: It indicates that parking is prohibited in the area.
Explanation: Parking is not permitted in the area, and offenders may be subject to penalties or towing, according to a rectangular sign with a white background and black letters or symbols, a red circle, and the words "no parking."

8. What do the words "merge" and a yellow diamond symbol in the middle of a rectangular sign with a white backdrop and black letters or symbols mean?
Answer: It denotes the merging of two lanes of traffic.
Explanation: Two lanes of traffic are merging into one when a rectangular sign with a white background and black letters or symbols, a yellow diamond symbol in the middle, and the words "merge," is displayed. The open lane should be used by drivers, and they should be aware of the impending slower traffic.

9. What does a circular sign that features a black image of a car sliding on a white backdrop with a red border mean?
Answer: It serves as a warning of slick or rainy driving conditions.
Explanation: A warning of slick or wet road conditions is displayed on a circular sign with a red border, a black image of a car skidding, and a white backdrop. Drivers should slow down and give themselves more room to maneuver.

10. What does a rectangular sign with a blue circle and the words "hospital" or a white letter "H" on a white backdrop with black text or symbols denote?
Answer: It indicates the location of a hospital or medical facility.
Explanation: The location of a hospital or medical institution is indicated by a rectangular sign with a white backdrop and black letters or symbols, along with the words "hospital" or a white letter "H" on a blue background.

Safe driving practices, pedestrians, and bicyclists
1. What should you do if a pedestrian is attempting to cross a road without a designated crosswalk or junction while you are driving?
Answer: In order to prevent an accident, you should give the pedestrian the right of way and drive carefully.
Explanation: Even in the absence of a clearly defined crosswalk or junction, pedestrians have the right of way on the road. In order to avoid an accident, drivers should yield to pedestrians and drive carefully.

2. What should you do if you are driving on a small road with no bike lane and a cyclist is coming at you from the opposite direction?
Answer: When passing a biker, go slowly and give them as much room as you can.
Explanation: On a small road without a bike lane, cars should allow bicyclists as much room as possible while overtaking them. Bicyclists have the right to utilize the roadway.

3. What should you do if a person is crossing the street against the flow of traffic while you are driving?
Answer: In order to prevent an accident, you should give the pedestrian the right of way and drive carefully.
Explanation: Even while walking against the flow of traffic, pedestrians have the right of way on the road. In order to avoid an accident, drivers should yield to pedestrians and drive carefully.

4. What should you do if you need to make a right turn while driving and a cyclist is cycling in the bike lane to your right?
Answer: When turning, you should provide a turn signal and only enter the bike lane when it is appropriate to do so.
Explanation: Motorists should be alert to cyclists' movements to prevent collisions. Bicyclists have the right to utilize bike lanes. Drivers should signal their purpose to turn before making a right turn, and they should only enter the bike lane when it is safe to do so.

5. What should you do if you're driving and a pedestrian using a service animal crosses the street?
Answer: You should be careful to prevent collisions and give the pedestrian and service animal the right of way.
Explanation: Even while walking beside a service animal, pedestrians have the right of way on the road. Drivers should use caution to prevent collisions and yield to pedestrians and service animals.

6. When should a motorist give way to a cyclist?
Answer: When a cyclist is in a bike lane, crossing the street, or entering the street from a driveway, you must surrender the right of way.
Explanation: On the road, bikers have the same rights and obligations as drivers. When a cyclist is in a bike lane, crossing the street, approaching the street from a driveway, or any other of these situations, drivers must yield to them.

7. What should you do if you're driving and a pedestrian using a white cane or a guiding dog is crossing the street?
Answer: In order to prevent an accident, you should give the pedestrian the right of way and drive carefully.
Explanation: People who are blind or visually impaired have the right-of-way on the road, and they frequently have a white cane or a guide dog with them. In order to avoid an accident, drivers should yield to pedestrians and drive carefully.

8. What should you do if a bicycle is riding in front of you while you are driving and is flashing a left turn signal?
Answer: is yes, but it's important to remember that you're not the only one who's going to be using this place.
Explanation: Drivers and bicyclists both have the right to use the road, and drivers should be alert to their movements to prevent accidents. Drivers should slow down, allow cyclists plenty of room, and wait to pass until they have finished their turn while they are signaling a left.

9. What should you do if a pedestrian is using a mobile device while walking on the road while you are driving?
Answer: Since a pedestrian might not be aware of their surroundings, you should give them the right of way and drive carefully to avoid an accident.
Explanation: Even if they are distracted by a mobile device and may not be aware of their surroundings, pedestrians have the right of way on the road. In order to avoid an accident, drivers should yield to pedestrians and drive carefully.

10. What should you do if you need to make a left turn and a cyclist is riding in the bike lane to your left while you are driving?

Answer: You should only merge into the bike lane when it is safe to do so, and you should yield to any bicyclists before making a turn.
Explanation: Motorists should be alert to cyclists' movements to prevent collisions. Bicyclists have the right to utilize bike lanes. In order to prevent cutting off bicyclists or colliding with them, cars should only enter into the bike lane when it is safe to do so when making a left turn.

Alcohol and drug awareness
1. What are the legal repercussions of marijuana use while driving in California?
Answer: Driving while intoxicated with marijuana is prohibited in California and carries the same penalties as driving while intoxicated with other narcotics or alcohol.
Explanation: Driving while intoxicated with marijuana is prohibited in California and carries the same fines, license suspension, and potential jail time as driving while intoxicated with other narcotics or alcohol.

2. In California, what are the legal repercussions of using bath salts while driving?
Answer: Driving while impaired by bath salts is prohibited in the state of California and may carry penalties comparable to those for driving while impaired by other drugs or alcohol.
Explanation: Driving under the influence of bath salts is prohibited in California and carries the same fines, license suspension, and potential jail time as driving under the influence of other drugs or alcohol.

3. How does alcohol affect a person's eyesight and sense of depth?
Answer: Drinking alcohol can impair eyesight and depth perception, making it challenging to effectively evaluate distances and recognize visual clues.
Explanation: Drinking alcohol can impair eyesight and depth perception, making it harder to evaluate distances effectively and recognize visual cues, increasing the likelihood

of accidents or other risky circumstances.

4. In California, what are the legal repercussions of driving while high on heroin?
Answer: Driving while under the influence of heroin is prohibited in California and carries the same penalties as driving while intoxicated by other substances.
Explanation: Driving under the influence of heroin is prohibited in California and carries the same fines, license suspension, and potential jail time as driving under the influence of other narcotics or alcohol.

5. How can distraction affect a person's ability to drive?
Answer: Distraction can make it harder for someone to drive since it diverts their focus from the road and slows down their reflexes.
Explanation: It's critical to avoid distractions when driving since they can damage a person's ability to drive by diverting their focus from the road and slowing down their reaction time.

6. In California, what are the legal repercussions of driving while under the influence of alcohol and drugs?
Answer: It's against the law to drive in California while under the influence of both drugs and alcohol. Penalties for this offense are the same as for driving while under the influence of just one of them.
Explanation: Driving while under the influence of both alcohol and drugs is prohibited in California and carries the same fines, license suspension, and potential jail time as driving while under the influence of just one of the substances.

7. How does alcohol affect a person's balance and coordination?
Answer: Drinking alcohol might make it challenging to carry out jobs that call on fine motor skills since it affects coordination and balance.
Explanation: Drinking alcohol can affect a person's balance and coordination, making it challenging to

do jobs that call on fine motor skills, like driving a car.

8. In California, what are the legal repercussions of driving while high on cocaine?
Answer: Driving while impaired by cocaine is banned in California and carries the same penalties as driving while impaired by other drugs or alcohol.
Explanation: Driving under the influence of cocaine is prohibited in California and carries the same fines, license suspension, and potential jail time as driving under the influence of other narcotics or alcohol.

9. How can anger or violent conduct affect a person's ability to drive?
Answer: Anger or violent conduct can make it more likely for someone to drive recklessly or aggressively, which impairs their ability to drive.
Explanation: It's vital to deal with anger or aggressive behavior before driving since it might make it more likely that someone would drive recklessly or aggressively.

10. In California, what are the legal repercussions of driving while under the influence of ecstasy?
Answer: Driving when impaired by ecstasy is prohibited in the state of California and may carry penalties comparable to those for driving while intoxicated by other substances or alcohol.
Explanation: Driving under the influence of ecstasy is prohibited in California and carries the same fines, license suspension, and potential jail time as driving under the influence of other drugs or alcohol.

Vehicle operation and maintenance
1. What function does an automobile's alternator serve?
Answer: The purpose of a car's alternator is to charge the battery and power the electrical systems of the vehicle while the engine is running.

Explanation: A car's alternator is an electrical component that produces power to charge the battery and run the car's electrical systems while the engine is operating.

2. How frequently should tires on an automobile be rotated?
Answer: Depending on the make and model of the automobile, the recommended tire rotation time might be anywhere from 5 and 7 miles.
Explanation: To maintain even wear and increase tire longevity, rotating a car's tires requires moving them from one position to another. Depending on the make and model of the vehicle, the recommended tire rotation time might range from 5,000 to 7,500 miles.

3. What does a car's timing belt serve?
Answer: A timing belt's job is to coordinate the crankshaft and camshaft rotations of an engine in order to maintain correct engine timing and performance.
Explanation: A car's timing belt joins the crankshaft and camshaft of the engine, ensuring that they rotate in unison and upholding correct engine timing and performance.

4. How frequently should spark plugs be changed in a car?
Answer: The suggested period for replacing a car's spark plugs varies based on the make and model of the vehicle, but generally speaking, it falls between 3 and 0 to 0 to 1 million miles.
Explanation: Spark plugs are a crucial part of an automobile's ignition system because they light the gasoline in the engine's cylinders. Depending on the make and type of the vehicle, the recommended replacement period normally ranges from 30,000 to 100,000 kilometers.

5. What are power windows on a car used for?
Answer: Power windows in cars are designed to make it easier and more

comfortable for the driver and passengers to raise or lower the windows with the press of a button.
Explanation: Power windows are an optional feature that enhances comfort and convenience by enabling the driver and passengers to raise or lower the windows at the push of a button.

6. How frequently should brake pads be changed on a car?
Answer: The recommended interval for replacing a car's brake pads varies depending on the make and model of the car, but typically ranges from 25,000 to 70,000 miles.
Explanation: The brake system of a car relies heavily on its brake pads, which are what slow down and stop the automobile. Depending on the make and type of the vehicle, the recommended replacement period normally ranges from 25,000 to 70,000 kilometers.

7. What does an automobile's exhaust system serve?
Answer: The function of an automobile's exhaust system is to remove dangerous gases and pollutants from the engine and discharge them outside of the car.
Explanation: To enhance air quality and minimize air pollution, a car's exhaust system removes dangerous gases and pollutants from the engine and exhales them outside the vehicle.

8. How frequently should a car's battery be replaced?
Answer: Depending on the make and model of the automobile, the suggested battery replacement frequency might be anywhere from 3 and 5 years.
Explanation: A car's battery is in charge of supplying energy for the electrical systems and starting the engine. Depending on the make and model of the automobile, the recommended time between replacements is normally between 3 and 5 years.

9. What does a car's differential fluid serve?
Answer: A car's differential fluid serves to lubricate the differential and lessen component wear and tear.
Explanation: A car's differential is in charge of dispersing force across the wheels and enabling them to rotate at various speeds during turns. As a lubricant, the differential fluid assists in minimizing component wear and tear.

10. How frequently should a car's fuel pump be replaced?
Answer: The recommended interval for replacing a car's fuel pump varies depending on the make and model of the car, but typically ranges from 70,000 to 100,000 miles.
Explanation: A car's fuel pump is in charge of transferring gasoline from the gas tank to the engine. Depending on the make and type of the automobile, the suggested replacement period varies, but is normally between 70,000 and 100,000 kilometers.

Emergency situations and procedures

1. What should you do if a tire on your car blows out while you're driving?
Answer: If you're driving and a tire blows out, you should maintain a tight grip on the steering wheel, let off the gas pedal gradually, and guide the car toward a safe place to stop.
Explanation: When a tire on your car blows out, the car could swerve and be challenging to manage. Hold the wheel firmly, ease off the throttle, and direct the car to a safe stop spot to reduce the chance of an accident.

2. What should you do if your car's engine overheats while you're driving?
Answer: If you are driving and the engine of your car overheats, you should switch on the heater to remove heat from the engine, turn off the air conditioner, and then stop in a safe place to allow the engine cool down before adding coolant.

Explanation: If the engine of your car overheats, it might harm the engine and raise the possibility of a breakdown. switch off the air conditioner and switch on the heater to remove heat from the engine to reduce the chance of further damage. Then, pull over to a safe spot and wait for the engine to cool before adding coolant.

3. What actions should you take if you see two cars colliding?
Answer: If you see two vehicles collide, contact 911 to report the accident and, if you can, help any wounded people.
Explanation: It's critical to alert emergency services right away if you see an accident involving two automobiles. As you wait for emergency personnel to come, you might be able to help any injured people.

4. If you are the first person on the scene of an accident, what should you do?
Answer: If you are the first person on the scene of an accident, you should dial 911 to report the accident and, if feasible, help any injured people.
Explanation: If you are the first person on the scene of an accident, you should call emergency services as quickly as you can. As you wait for emergency personnel to come, you might be able to help any injured people.

5. What should you do if you notice emergency vehicles with lights and sirens coming up behind you while driving?
Answer: If you are driving and you notice an emergency vehicle coming at you from behind, pull over to the right side of the road and wait until it passes.
Explanation: It's crucial to yield to emergency vehicles with lights and sirens if you notice them coming from behind so they can attend to the situation as fast as possible.

6. What should you do if you encounter a person crossing the street at an unidentified crosswalk while driving?
Answer: If you are driving and you notice a pedestrian crossing the street at an unmarked crosswalk, you should stop and let them cross safely.
Explanation: To guarantee a pedestrian's safety, it is necessary to yield to them when they are crossing the street at an unmarked crosswalk.

7. What should you do if a school bus with flashing red lights and an extended stop sign crosses your path while you are driving?
Answer: If you are driving and come across a school bus with flashing red lights and an extended stop sign, you should pull over at least 20 feet away from the vehicle and wait for the lights and stop sign to turn off before moving on.
Explanation: If a school bus has flashing red lights and an extended stop sign, it is forbidden to pass because children are getting on or off the bus. It's crucial to halt at least 20 feet away from the bus and to wait until the stop sign and lights have been switched off before moving on.

8. What should you do if you notice a car with warning lights on the side of the road while you are driving?
Answer: If you are driving and you come across a car with hazard lights on the side of the road, you should shift over to the next lane if you can and slow down to allow the car and its passengers some room.
Explanation: If a car is stopped by the side of the road with its hazard lights on, it can be having a mechanical issue or a crisis. If feasible, move over to the next lane and slow down to allow enough room for the car and its occupants.

9. What should you do if you encounter a bike or pedestrian on the road while you are driving?
Answer: When passing a bike or pedestrian in the road while driving,

slow down and allow them plenty of room.
Explanation: In order to ensure their safety, it is crucial to allow pedestrians and cyclists enough of room when passing. They are more vulnerable than automobiles.

10. What should you do if you come across a flooded road while driving?
Answer: If you're driving and you encounter a flooded road, you should reverse and seek out an alternative route. As it may be challenging to determine the level of the water and as a result cause your car to stall or be swept away, do not attempt to drive across the flooded roads.
Explanation: Driving across a flooded roadway is particularly risky since it increases the chance that your car may stall or get swept away by the river. To secure your safety and the safety of others, you must back up and choose a different path.

Practice Test 6:
Traffic laws, Driving rules and regulations
1. How fast are cars allowed to go on a Californian street in a neighborhood close to a school?
Answer: 25 miles per hour
Explanation: Unless otherwise marked, the top speed restriction for cars traveling down a California street in a neighborhood close to a school is 25 miles per hour.

2. What should you do if you're driving along a street in California when you observe a pedestrian using a clearly designated crosswalk to cross the roadway?
Answer: Reverse your direction and give the pedestrian the right-of-way.
Explanation: If you are driving on a roadway in California and you notice a person crossing the street at a clearly designated crosswalk, you must stop your car and give the pedestrian the right-of-way.

3. When approaching a railroad crossing in California with flashing warning lights, what is the top speed restriction for moving vehicles?
Answer: 15 miles per hour
Explanation: In California, when approaching a railroad crossing with flashing warning lights, a vehicle's top speed restriction is 15 miles per hour.

4. What should you do if you encounter a sign signaling a merge ahead while traveling on a Californian highway?
Answer: Move into the lane designated by the sign, and then reduce your speed.
Explanation: If you are on a California highway when a sign warning of a merge appears, you should merge into that lane and reduce your speed in accordance with the notice's instructions.

5. On two-lane undivided roads or in certain rural parts of California, what is the top speed limit for moving vehicles?
Answer: 65 miles per hour
Explanation: Unless otherwise specified, the top speed limit for cars traveling on a California roadway in some rural regions or on two-lane undivided highways is 65 miles per hour.

6. What should you do if you're driving down a roadway in California and you come across a person using an unmarked crosswalk?
Answer: Reverse your direction and give the pedestrian the right-of-way.
Explanation: If you're driving along a street in California and you observe a pedestrian crossing the roadway in a spot that isn't marked as a crosswalk, you have to stop and give them the right-of-way.

7. When approaching a school crossing when kids are crossing the street, what is the top speed restriction for cars on a Californian street?
Answer: 25 miles per hour
Explanation: When approaching a school crossing in California when kids are crossing the street, the top

speed restriction for cars is 25 miles per hour.

8. What should you do if you encounter a bicycle lane with strong white lines while driving along a Californian street?
Answer: Avoid using the bicycle lane for motor vehicles and give bicycles in the lane the right-of-way.
Explanation: If you are driving on a street in California and you notice a bicycle lane with solid white lines, you must not drive in the lane and give way to any bicycles who are riding in it.

9. When passing a school building or grounds with kids playing outside or crossing the street, what is the top speed restriction for cars on a Californian street?
Answer: 25 miles per hour
Explanation: In California, the speed restriction for cars passing a school's building or grounds while kids are playing outdoors or crossing the street is 25 miles per hour.

10. What should you do if you notice a sign indicating a construction zone ahead while travelling on a Californian highway?
Answer: Reduce speed and be ready to stop, obey any traffic control directives issued by construction workers, and merge into the proper lane as soon as it is safe to do so.
Explanation: If you are traveling in California and you notice a sign warning you that there is a work zone ahead, you should slow down and be ready to stop, heed any directions provided by construction personnel, and move into the designated lane as soon as it is safe to do so.

Road signs and signals
1. What does a rectangular sign with a green circle and the words "exit only" or an arrow pointing to the right, with a black backdrop and letters or symbols, mean?
Answer: It designates a lane that may be used to turn right or leave the road.

Explanation: A rectangular sign with a white backdrop and black wording or symbols, together with a green circle and the words "exit only" or an arrow pointing to the right, designates a lane for leaving the road or making a right turn.

2. What does a rectangular sign that reads "no trucks" and has a red circle and slash across it, with a white backdrop and black wording or symbols, mean?
Answer: It means that trucks or other commercial vehicles are not permitted on the route.
Explanation: A rectangular sign with a white backdrop, black letters or symbols, a red circle and slash across it, and the phrase "no trucks" denotes that commercial vehicles and trucks are not permitted on the route. Alternative routes must be found by truck truckers.

3. What does a rectangular sign with a red circle and slash across it and the words "no parking or standing" mean? It has a white backdrop and black wording or symbols.
Answer: It means that standing or parking is not allowed in the area.
Explanation: A rectangular sign with a white backdrop and black letters or symbols, a red circle and slash across it, and the phrase "no parking or standing," signifies that parking or standing is forbidden in the area and that offenders may be fined or have their vehicles towed.

4. What does a rectangular sign with a green circle and the words "pedestrian crossing" in black letters or symbols on a white backdrop mean?
Answer: It indicates a designated crossing area for pedestrians.
Explanation: A rectangular sign with a green circle and the words "pedestrian crossing," written in black letters or symbols on a white backdrop designates a pedestrian crossing. Drivers should slow down and yield to pedestrians if possible.

5. What does a rectangular sign that says "end construction zone" and has a yellow diamond symbol in the middle and black letters or symbols indicate?
Answer: It indicates the end of a construction zone.
Explanation: A rectangular sign with a white backdrop and black letters or symbols, a yellow diamond symbol in the middle, and the words "end construction zone," marks the conclusion of a construction zone. Drivers should get back to their regular driving routine.

6. What does a circular sign that says "railroad crossing" and has the initials "RR" in it and a red border mean?
Answer: It indicates the presence of a railroad crossing ahead.
Explanation: There is a railroad crossing ahead, indicated by a circular sign with a white backdrop and a red border that says "railroad crossing" and the initials "RR." Drivers ought to reduce their speed and be ready to stop if required.

7. What do the words "bus lane" or a bus emblem on a rectangular sign with a green circle and a white backdrop and black letters or symbols mean?
Answer: It indicates a designated lane for buses.
Explanation: There is a dedicated lane for buses where there is a rectangular sign with a white backdrop and black letters or symbols, a green circle, and the words "bus lane" or a bus symbol. When a bus is merging into traffic, drivers should yield and should not drive in this lane unless they are making a right turn.

8. What does a rectangular sign that says "divided highway ends" and has a yellow diamond symbol in the center and black wording or symbols indicate?
Answer: It indicates the end of a divided highway, where traffic will be merging into a single lane.
Explanation: At the conclusion of a split highway, when traffic will merge into a single lane, a rectangular sign with a white background and black letters or symbols, a yellow diamond symbol in the middle, and the words "divided highway ends," will be present. Drivers should reduce their speed and be ready for traffic that is merging.

9. What does a rectangular sign with a red circle and slash across it and the words "no turn on red" mean? It has a white backdrop and black wording or symbols.
Answer: It means that going right or left on a red signal at the intersection is not permitted.
Explanation: A rectangular sign with a white backdrop, black letters or symbols, a red circle and slash across it, and the phrase "no turn on red" denotes that turning right or left on a red light at the junction is not permitted. Prior to making the turn, drivers must wait for a green light.

10. What does a rectangular sign with a green circle and the words "milepost" or a number indicate? It has a white backdrop with black wording or symbols.
Answer: It gives the mileage starting from a certain location on the route.
Explanation: The number of miles from a certain location on the road is indicated by a rectangular sign with a white background and black letters or symbols, a green circle, and the words "milepost" or a number. These markers are used for navigation and calculating distance.

Safe driving practices, pedestrians, and bicyclists
1. What should you do if you're driving and a pedestrian is using a crosswalk that is clearly marked and equipped with a traffic light to cross the street?
Answer: Even if you have a green light or an arrow, you must yield to the pedestrian and stop at the red light or stop sign.
Explanation: Even if there is a green light or arrow, cars must stop at the red light or stop sign and yield to

pedestrians in defined crosswalks with traffic signals.

2. What should you do if you need to parallel park your car but a cyclist is riding in the bike lane to your right while you are driving?
Answer: You should scan for approaching bicycles, indicate your intentions, and only merge into the bike lane when it is safe to do so.
Explanation: Motorists should be alert to cyclists' movements to prevent collisions. Bicyclists have the right to utilize bike lanes. Drivers should scan for approaching cyclists before parallel parking, give them plenty of room, and only merge into the bike lane when it's safe to do so.

3. What should you do if a person is crossing the street at night while wearing dark clothing?
Answer: To prevent an accident, you should drive more slowly and cautiously. If required, you can also turn on your high lights to improve visibility.
Explanation: Motorists should use caution to prevent collisions since pedestrians on the road have the right of way. In the event that a pedestrian is wearing dark apparel at night, motorists should slow down and, if required, turn on their high lights to improve visibility.

4. What should you do if a bike is moving slowly in front of you while you are driving?
Answer: You should pass a biker only when it is safe to do so, slow down, and allow them plenty of room.
Explanation: Drivers and bicyclists both have the right to use the road, and drivers should be alert to their movements to prevent accidents. Drivers should slow down, allow bicyclists enough of room, and only pass them when it is safe to do so while they are moving slowly.

5. What should you do if a person pushing a stroller carrying a child crosses your path while you are driving?

Answer: You should give the pedestrian the right-of-way, drive carefully to avoid collisions, and pay attention to the child's actions.
Explanation: Drivers should use caution to prevent collisions on the road since pedestrians pushing strollers have the right of way. In order to prevent an accident, drivers should be mindful of the child's actions and use additional caution.

6. What should you do if a cyclist is riding in a bike lane to your right while you are driving and the bike lane ends?
Answer: Before reversing into the traffic lane, move into the bike lane and give way to the cyclist.
Explanation: Motorists should be alert to cyclists' movements to prevent collisions. Bicyclists have the right to utilize bike lanes. When a bike lane comes to an end, motorists should re-enter the road after merging into the bike lane and giving way to cyclists.

7. What should you do if you're driving and a person in a wheelchair is crossing the street?
Answer: You should be careful to prevent collisions and give the wheelchair and pedestrian the right of way.
Explanation: Drivers should use caution to prevent collisions since pedestrians using wheelchairs have the right of way on the road. In order to prevent an accident, drivers should be mindful of the wheelchair's movements and use extreme caution.

8. What should you do if you need to make a right turn while driving and a cyclist is cycling in the bike lane to your left?
Answer: You should only merge into the bike lane when it is safe to do so, and you should yield to any bicyclists before making a turn.
Explanation: Motorists should be alert to cyclists' movements to prevent collisions. Bicyclists have the right to utilize bike lanes. Drivers should merge into the bike lane only when it is safe to do so and yield to the

bicycle before making their turn if they are making a right turn and a cyclist is riding in the bike lane to their left.

9. What should you do if you're driving and a pedestrian is using a walker or crutches to cross the street?
Answer: In order to prevent a collision, you should yield to pedestrians and drive carefully. You should also be aware of the pedestrian's actions and any possible dangers.
Explanation: Drivers should use caution to prevent collisions as pedestrians using walkers or crutches have the right of way on the road. The motions of the pedestrian and any possible dangers, such as abrupt stops or turns, should be observed by the driver as well.

10. What should you do if you need to perform a U-turn while driving and a cyclist is cycling in the bike lane to your right?
Answer: You should only merge into the bike lane when it is safe to do so, and you must yield to any bicyclists before making a U-turn.
Explanation: Motorists should be alert to cyclists' movements to prevent collisions. Bicyclists have the right to utilize bike lanes. Drivers should merge into the bike lane only when it is safe to do so and yield to the biker before performing their U-turn if a cyclist is riding in the bike lane to their right and you are making a turn.

Alcohol and drug awareness
1. In California, what are the legal repercussions of refusing to submit to an alcohol or drug test via chemical means?
Answer: It's against the law and subject to fines, license suspension, and other sanctions in California to refuse to submit to a chemical test for drugs or alcohol.
Explanation: It is against the law in California to refuse to submit to a chemical test for alcohol or drugs, and doing so can result in fines,

license suspensions, and required DUI education programs, among other sanctions.

2. How does alcohol affect a person's capacity for judgment and decision-making?
Answer: yes, but it's important to remember that you can't always get what you're looking for when you're in the middle of a crisis.
Explanation: It's crucial to refrain from drinking alcohol while operating a car since it can impair judgment and decision-making skills, which can result in bad judgments and increased risk-taking behavior.

3. What are the legal repercussions of driving while impaired by prescription medication in California?
Answer: Driving under the influence of prescription medications is prohibited in California and carries the same penalties as driving under the influence of other substances or alcohol.
Explanation: Driving under the influence of prescription medicines is prohibited in California and carries the same fines, license suspension, and potential jail time as driving under the influence of illicit substances or alcohol.

4. How does marijuana affect a person's ability to drive?
Answer: Marijuana can make it harder to drive since it affects judgment, response time, and coordination.
Explanation: It's crucial to avoid smoking marijuana while driving since it can make a person less coordinated, slower to respond, and less judgmental.

5. In California, what are the legal repercussions of using a fake ID to buy alcohol?
Answer: It's against the law to use a fraudulent ID to buy alcohol in California, and doing so might result in fines, community service, and other sanctions.

Explanation: In California, using a fake ID to buy alcohol is prohibited and is punishable by fines, community service, and attendance at an alcohol education program.

6. How does weariness affect a person's response time?
Answer: Being tired might make it harder for a driver to react quickly to unforeseen events.
Explanation: Being tired makes it harder to react quickly to unexpected events when driving, which raises the chance of accidents.

7. In California, what are the legal repercussions of driving while high on synthetic drugs?
Answer: Driving while impaired by synthetic substances is prohibited in the state of California and may carry penalties comparable to those for driving while impaired by other drugs or alcohol.
Explanation: Driving under the influence of synthetic substances is prohibited in California and carries the same fines, license suspension, and potential jail time as driving under the influence of other drugs or alcohol.

8. How does alcohol affect a person's capacity to recognize and react to visual cues?
Answer: Drinking alcohol can affect one's perception of and reaction to visual signals, making it more challenging to effectively evaluate distances and respond to unexpected events.
Explanation: Drinking alcohol can impair a person's perception of and reaction to visual signals, making it harder to effectively gauge distances and respond to unexpected events, raising the risk of accidents.

9. In California, what are the legal repercussions of driving while high on methadone?
Answer: Driving while under the influence of methadone is against the law in California and carries the same punishments as driving when intoxicated by other substances or alcohol.
Explanation: Driving under the influence of methadone is prohibited in California and carries the same fines, license suspension, and potential jail time as driving under the influence of other narcotics or alcohol.

10. How does distraction affect a person's capacity to keep a safe following distance?
Answer: Distraction can make it more difficult for a driver to keep a safe following distance since it diverts their focus from the road and slows down their reflexes.
Explanation: Distractions when driving should be avoided since they can damage a person's ability to keep a safe following distance by diverting their attention from the road and slowing down their reaction time.

Vehicle operation and maintenance

1. What does a catalytic converter do in a car?
Answer: The catalytic converter in a car is designed to cut down on dangerous pollutants like carbon monoxide, nitrogen oxides, and hydrocarbons that are released by the engine.
Explanation: A car's catalytic converter reduces emissions by using a chemical reaction to change toxic engine pollutants into less damaging ones like carbon dioxide, water vapor, and nitrogen.

2. How frequently should a serpentine belt be changed on a car?
Answer: Depending on the make and model of the automobile, the suggested time for serpentine belt replacement varies, but it normally falls between 60,000 and 100,000 miles.
Explanation: The alternator, power steering pump, and air conditioning compressor are just a few of the engine's parts that are driven by a car's serpentine belt. Depending on the make and type of the automobile,

the suggested replacement period varies, but is normally between 60,000 and 100,000 kilometers.

3. What does a car's power steering system serve?
Answer: The power steering system in a car helps the driver steer by making it easier to spin the wheel and by giving the driver more control and precision.
Explanation: A car's power steering system is intended to help the driver steer the automobile by making it simpler to spin the wheel and granting more control and accuracy. Utilizing hydraulic or electric power support allows for this.

4. How frequently should a car's timing belt be replaced?
Answer: The recommended interval for replacing a car's timing belt varies depending on the make and model of the car, but typically ranges from 60,000 to 100,000 miles.
Explanation: A crucial part of the engine that synchronizes the rotation of the crankshaft and camshaft is the timing belt in an automobile. Depending on the make and type of the automobile, the suggested replacement period varies, but is normally between 60,000 and 100,000 kilometers.

5. What does an automobile's air conditioning system serve?
Answer: The purpose of a car's air conditioning system is to cool and dehumidify the air inside the vehicle, providing greater comfort and reducing driver fatigue.
Explanation: A car's air conditioning system is made to chill and dehumidify the inside air, enhancing comfort for the driver and passengers while lowering fatigue and distraction levels in the driver.

6. How frequently should an automobile's engine air filter be changed?
Answer: The suggested time for replacing a car's engine air filter varies based on the make and model of the vehicle, but generally speaking, it's between 1 and 5 miles (or 1 to 0).
Explanation: To prevent harm to the engine and maintain peak performance, the engine air filter of a car is in charge of collecting dirt, dust, and other impurities from the air entering the engine. Depending on the make and type of the automobile, the suggested replacement period might vary, although it normally falls between 15,000 and 30,000 kilometers.

7. What does a gasoline filter on an automobile do?
Answer: A fuel filter's job is to filter out impurities from fuel before it reaches an engine, preventing harm and ensuring peak performance.
Explanation: A car's gasoline filter is made to filter out debris, rust, and other impurities before the fuel reaches the engine, preventing damage and ensuring maximum performance.

8. How frequently should transmission fluid be changed in a car?
Answer: Depending on the make and model of the vehicle, the recommended interval for refilling the transmission fluid varies from 3 0 0 to 6 0 0 miles.
Explanation: A car's transmission fluid is in charge of lubricating, cooling, and pressurizing the hydraulic system used to change gears. Depending on the make and type of the automobile, the suggested replacement period might vary, although it normally falls between 30,000 and 60,000 kilometers.

9. What does a tire pressure monitoring system in an automobile do?
Answer: A tire pressure monitoring system in a car alerts the driver when a tire's pressure is low, helping to avoid tire damage and enhancing safety and fuel economy.
Explanation: A car's tire pressure monitoring system is intended to warn the driver when the tire

pressure is low, preventing tire damage and enhancing safety and fuel economy.

10. How frequently should an oxygen sensor in an automobile be replaced?
Answer: Depending on the make and model of the vehicle, the recommended mileage between oxygen sensor replacements varies from 6 1 0 0 to 6 1 0 miles.
Explanation: An automobile's oxygen sensor measures the quantity of oxygen present in exhaust gases and relays this information to the engine control module, which then modifies the air/fuel ratio for optimum performance and emissions. Depending on the make and type of the automobile, the suggested replacement period varies, but is normally between 60,000 and 100,000 kilometers.

Emergency situations and procedures
1. What should you do if you suddenly lose your ability to stop while driving?
Answer: If you suddenly lose control of your brakes while driving, maneuver the car to a safe area to come to a halt while using the emergency brake and a lower gear.
Explanation: It may be challenging to stop the car if you suddenly lose your brakes. The chance of a collision can be reduced by navigating to a safe spot to stop the car, downshifting to a lower gear, and using the emergency brake.

2. What should you do if your car starts to hydroplane while you're driving?
Answer: If you're driving and you see that your car is beginning to hydroplane, you should let off the accelerator, keep going straight, and wait for the tires to regain traction before using the brakes or making a turn.
Explanation: When water accumulates on the road, hydroplaning happens when the tires lose touch with it. To reduce the

chance of an accident, let off the throttle slowly, drive straight ahead, and hold off on braking or turning until the tires have gained traction again.

3. What should you do if your car's accelerator pedal becomes stuck while you're driving?
Answer: If you're driving and the accelerator pedal on your car becomes stuck, you should put the car in neutral, apply the brakes to slow it down, and steer to a safe place to stop it.
Explanation: If the accelerator pedal of your car gets stuck, the car could accelerate suddenly. The vehicle may be made to go more slowly and come to a stop by shifting into neutral and disengaging the engine from the wheels.

4. What should you do if you smell smoke coming from your car while driving or see flames rising from it?
Answer: If you are driving and you smell smoke or see flames coming from your car, stop in a safe place, switch off the engine, and get out of the car right away.
Explanation: If smoke or flames are flowing from your car, there may be a fire inside, which is quite dangerous. It's crucial to stop in a secure area, turn off the engine, and get out of the car as soon as you can.

5. What should you do if your car's hood suddenly pops up and obstructs your vision while you're driving?
Answer: If you are driving and your vehicle's hood suddenly flies up and blocks your view, you should look through the gap at the bottom of the hood, slow down, and steer to a safe location to stop the vehicle.
Explanation: It might be challenging to see the road ahead if your car's hood unexpectedly pops up and obstructs your vision. You can see the road better by looking through the bottom of the hood's gap, and you can reduce the likelihood of an accident by slowing down and

directing the car to a safe place to stop.

6. What should you do if you lose power steering while driving?
Answer: If you are driving and lose power steering, you should maintain a tight hold on the steering wheel, apply additional force as you turn it, and drive the car to a safe place to stop.
Explanation: Losing power steering might make it harder to control the direction of the car. The loss of power steering can be made up for by gripping the steering wheel firmly, turning with additional force, and guiding the car to a safe stop to reduce the chance of an accident.

7. What should you do if you hear a loud noise coming from the engine of your car while you are driving?
Answer: To prevent additional damage, you should pull over to a safe spot and turn off your car's engine if you are driving and hear a loud noise coming from it.
Explanation: A loud noise emanating from your car's engine might be a sign of a significant issue, such a technical breakdown or an oil shortage. In order to prevent more damage or the possibility of a breakdown, it is crucial to stop the vehicle in a safe area and turn off the engine.

8. What should you do if you realize that the temperature gauge on your car is in the danger zone while you are driving?
Answer: If you are driving and you discover that your car's temperature gauge is in the danger zone, you should turn on the heater, switch off the air conditioning, and pull over to a safe place so that the engine can cool down before adding coolant.
Explanation: The engine may be overheating if the temperature gauge on your car is in the red zone. The chance of a breakdown can be reduced by putting on the heater and shutting off the air conditioner to assist remove heat from the engine.

You should also pull over to a safe area to allow the engine cool down before adding coolant.

9. What should you do if you see that the oil pressure indicator on your car is low while you are driving?
Answer: If you are driving and you discover that the oil pressure gauge on your car is low, you should pull over to a safe spot and turn off the engine to prevent further damage or the possibility of an accident. If required, check the oil level and add oil.
Explanation: A low oil pressure indicator might mean that the engine isn't getting adequate lubrication, which could harm it. In order to prevent more damage or the possibility of a breakdown, it is crucial to stop the vehicle in a safe area and turn off the engine. Before starting the engine again, check the oil level and add more if required.

10. What should you do if you see your car's battery warning light on while you're driving?
Answer: If you are driving and you notice that your car's battery warning light is on, you should switch off all non-essential electrical equipment, such as the radio and air conditioner, and proceed to a secure area to have the battery and charging system checked.
Explanation: A battery warning light might mean that the battery is not being charged properly, which could result in the vehicle losing power. Non-essential electrical equipment can be turned off to save battery power, and having the battery and charging system examined while moving to a safe area will help avoid a failure.

Practice Test 7:
Traffic laws, Driving rules and regulations
1. In the absence of posted speed limit signs, what is the top speed limit for cars traveling down a California street in a commercial or residential area?

Answer: 25 miles per hour
Explanation: If there are no posted speed limit signs on a California roadway in a commercial or residential area, the top speed restriction for moving vehicles is 25 miles per hour.

2. What should you do if a red traffic light is blinking while you are traveling along a street in California?
Answer: Stop your car, give way to other traffic and pedestrians, and move forward once it's safe to do so.
Explanation: When a flashing red traffic light is present on a California roadway, drivers are required to stop, give way to other cars and pedestrians, and then resume driving when it is safe to do so.

3. In metropolitan areas or close to schools, what is the top speed limit for automobiles traveling on a California highway?
Answer: 55 miles per hour
Explanation: Unless otherwise marked, the top speed restriction for cars traveling on a California highway in some metropolitan areas or close to schools is 55 miles per hour.

4. What should you do if you notice a yield sign while driving down a Californian street?
Answer: Move slowly, give oncoming traffic the right-of-way at the crossroads or crossroad, and drive carefully.
Explanation: If you notice a yield sign while driving along a California street, you must slow down, give the right-of-way to oncoming vehicles at the crossroads or crossroad, and drive cautiously.

5. On a California highway, what is the top speed limit for cars pulling a car or a trailer?
Answer: 55 miles per hour
Explanation: Unless otherwise indicated, the top speed limit for cars hauling a car or a trailer on a California roadway is 55 miles per hour.

6. What should you do if a traffic light is green and you're going down a street in California?
Answer: If the junction is clear, move forward, but always give way to oncoming traffic, including pedestrians and other cars.
Explanation: If a traffic signal is green while you are driving on a California street and the junction is clear, you should continue. However, you should always yield to any pedestrians or other vehicles that are still in the intersection.

7. What is the top speed limit for cars traveling down a residential street in California?
Answer: 25 miles per hour
Explanation: Unless otherwise marked, the top speed restriction for cars traveling along a street in a residential part of California is 25 miles per hour.

8. What should you do if you notice a sign warning of an approaching bend while traveling on a Californian highway?
Answer: Reduce your speed before the curve and then increase it afterwards.
Explanation: If you are traveling on a California highway and you notice a sign warning you of an approaching curve, you should slow down and modify your speed appropriately before entering the curve.

9. In a public park in California, what is the top speed restriction for moving cars?
Answer: 15 miles per hour
Explanation: In a public park in California, the top speed restriction for moving vehicles is 15 miles per hour.

10. What should you do if you notice a red traffic light while driving along a street in California?
Answer: Halt your car and keep it there until the signal turns green.
Explanation: If you are driving along a street in the state of California and you encounter a red traffic light, you

must stop and stay stopped until the light turns green.

Road signs and signals

1. What does a rectangular sign with a red circle and slash across it and the words "no U-turn" mean? It has a white backdrop and black wording or symbols.
Answer: It says that at the junction, a U-turn is not allowed.
Explanation: Making a U-turn at the junction is not allowed, as indicated by a rectangular sign with a white background and black letters or symbols, a red circle, a slash across it, and the words "no U-turn." Drivers need to find a another route.

2. What do the words "bicycle crossing" or a bicycle symbol on a rectangular sign with a green circle and a white backdrop and black letters or symbols mean?
Answer: It designates a bicycle-only crossing place.
Explanation: A rectangular sign indicating a designated bicycle crossing location has a white backdrop, black letters or symbols, a green circle, and either the words "bicycle crossing" or a bicycle symbol. Bicyclists should yield to traffic, and drivers should be ready to stop if required.

3. What does a rectangular sign that reads "road work ahead" and has a yellow diamond symbol in the middle and black letters or symbols on a white backdrop mean?
Answer: It suggests that there will be upcoming roadwork or construction.
Explanation: There will be road work or construction ahead, as indicated by a rectangular sign with a white background and black letters or symbols, a yellow diamond symbol in the middle, and the words "road work ahead." Drivers need to slow down and be ready for lane closures and detours.

4. What does a rectangular sign with a green circle and the words "emergency evacuation route" in black letters or symbols on a white backdrop mean?
Answer: It designates a specific evacuation path in case of emergency.
Explanation: A rectangular sign with a white backdrop and black letters or symbols, a green circle, and the words "emergency evacuation route," designates a path for an emergency evacuation. Drivers should be aware of these roads and, if required, give way to emergency vehicles.

5. What does a rectangular sign with a red circle and slash across it and the words "no right turn" mean? It has a white backdrop and black wording or symbols.
Answer: It means that turning right at the junction is not allowed.
Explanation: A rectangular sign with a white backdrop and black letters or symbols, a red circle and slash across it, and the phrase "no right turn" denotes that making a right turn at the junction is not permitted. Drivers need to find another route.

6. What does a circular sign that has a black image of a hand in the "stop" position against a white backdrop and red border mean?
Answer: It designates a crosswalk for pedestrians, and any vehicles approaching must stop if pedestrians are present.
Explanation: A circular sign with a white backdrop and red border, together with a black image of a hand in the "stop" position, designates a pedestrian crossing. If pedestrians are in the crosswalk, cars are required to stop. Drivers should slow down and yield to pedestrians if possible.

7. What do the words "disabled parking permit required" or a wheelchair emblem on a rectangular sign with a blue circle and a white backdrop and black letters or symbols mean?
Answer: It denotes a parking space reserved for cars with handicapped parking permits.

Explanation: A rectangular sign with a white background and black letters or symbols, together with a blue circle and the phrase "disabled parking permit required" or a symbol of a wheelchair, designates a parking space for cars with handicapped parking permits. Fines or towing may be imposed on offenders.

8. What does a rectangular sign that reads "lane ends" and has a yellow diamond symbol in the center and black letters or symbols on a white backdrop mean?
Answer: This sign denotes the point at which one lane ends and another begins.
Explanation: At the end of a lane, where traffic will merge into another, a rectangular sign with a white background and black letters or symbols, a yellow diamond symbol in the middle, and the words "lane ends," is shown. Drivers should reduce their speed and be ready for traffic that is merging.

9. What does a rectangular sign with "no stopping" written in red with a red circle and slash across it on a white backdrop and black letters or symbols denote?
Answer: It means that halting is not allowed in the region.
Explanation: A rectangular sign with a white backdrop and black letters or symbols, a red circle and slash across it, and the phrase "no stopping," denotes that halting is forbidden in the area and that violators may be liable to penalties or towing.

10. What does a circular sign that has a black image of a vehicle going up a hill with a red border and a white backdrop mean?
Answer: It serves as a warning that there is a hill or grade ahead.
Explanation: A circular sign warning of a steep grade or hill ahead has a black image of a truck on an incline against a white backdrop and red border. To stay in control and prevent brake failure, drivers should slow down and downshift.

Safe driving practices, pedestrians, and bicyclists

1. What should you do if you're driving and a pedestrian is using headphones or earphones while crossing the street?
Answer: Because the pedestrian might not be able to hear your car, you should drive carefully and be ready to stop.
Explanation: Drivers should use caution and be ready to stop if a pedestrian is using earbuds or headphones since they may not be able to hear your vehicle. Pedestrians also have the right of way on the road.

2. What should you do if you're driving and a bicycle in a commercial district is riding on the sidewalk?
Answer: Be cautious while passing pedestrians on the sidewalk and be aware that it's often not permitted to ride bicycles in commercial districts.
Explanation: Drivers should be aware of this regulation and use caution while overtaking people on the sidewalk. Bicycles are normally not permitted to be ridden on sidewalks in business districts.

3. What should you do if a person with a white cane and a red tip is crossing your path while you're driving?
Answer: The white cane and red tip of the walking stick are indicators that the pedestrian is blind or visually challenged, therefore you should yield to them and drive carefully to prevent an accident.
Explanation: People who are blind or visually impaired have the right-of-way on the road, and a white cane with a red tip is a sign that they are carrying this. These pedestrians should be given the right of way, and drivers should drive carefully to prevent collisions.

4. What should you do if you need to make a left turn while driving and a cyclist is cycling in the bike lane to your right?

Answer: You should only merge into the bike lane when it is safe to do so, and you should yield to any bicyclists before making a turn.
Explanation: Motorists should be alert to cyclists' movements to prevent collisions. Bicyclists have the right to utilize bike lanes. Drivers should merge into the bike lane only when it is safe to do so and yield to the bicycle before making their turn if they are making a left turn and a cyclist is riding in the bike lane to your right.

5. What should you do if you're driving and you see a person carrying a dog on a leash crossing the street?
Answer: You should be careful to prevent a collision and give the pedestrian and dog the right of way.
Explanation: Drivers should yield to pedestrians who are carrying dogs on the road and use caution to avoid an accident.

6. What should you do if you need to make a right turn while driving and a cyclist is cycling in the bike lane to your right?
Answer: When turning, you should provide a turn signal and only enter the bike lane when it is appropriate to do so.
Explanation: Motorists should be alert to cyclists' movements to prevent collisions. Bicyclists have the right to utilize bike lanes. Drivers should signal their purpose to turn while making a right turn and only enter the bike lane when it is safe to do so.

7. What should you do if a person is carrying a child as they cross the street while you're driving?
Answer: You should be careful to prevent an accident and give the pedestrian and youngster the right of way.
Explanation: Drivers should defer to pedestrians with children and use caution to prevent collisions since they have the right of way on the road.

8. What should you do if you need to perform a U-turn but a cyclist is riding in the bike lane to your right while you are driving?
Answer: You should only merge into the bike lane when it is safe to do so, and you must yield to any bicyclists before making a U-turn.
Explanation: Motorists should be alert to cyclists' movements to prevent collisions. Bicyclists have the right to utilize bike lanes. Drivers should merge into the bike lane only when it is safe to do so and yield to the biker before performing their U-turn if a cyclist is riding in the bike lane to their right and you are making a turn.

9. What should you do if you're driving and you see a person using a wheelchair or scooter to cross the street?
Answer: You should take care to avoid collisions and provide the pedestrian and mobility device the right of way.
Explanation: Drivers should yield to pedestrians using mobility aids and use caution to prevent collisions since they have the right of way on the road.

10. What should you do if a bicycle in front of you abruptly stops or swerves to avoid a hazard while you are driving?
Answer: You should go slower, provide enough of room for the bicycle, and be ready to stop or move to prevent a collision.
Explanation: Drivers and bicyclists both have the right to use the road, and drivers should be alert to their movements to prevent accidents. Drivers should slow down, allow cyclists enough of room, and be ready to stop or swerve to prevent a collision when they abruptly halt or swerve to avoid an obstruction.

Alcohol and drug awareness
1. In California, what are the legal repercussions of using hallucinogens while driving?
Answer: Driving while high on hallucinogens is prohibited in

California and carries the same penalties as driving when intoxicated by other drugs or alcohol.
Explanation: Driving while under the influence of hallucinogens is prohibited in California and carries the same fines, license suspension, and potential jail time as driving while under the influence of other drugs or alcohol.

2. How can alcohol affect a person's capacity for good judgment?
Answer: Drinking alcohol can decrease one's capacity to make wise decisions, which can result in poor judgment and greater risk-taking behavior.
Explanation: It's crucial to refrain from drinking alcohol while operating a car since it can impair one's capacity to make wise decisions, which can result in bad choices and greater risk-taking behavior.

3. In California, what are the legal repercussions of giving alcohol to a minor?
Answer: It's against the law to give alcohol to a child in California, and doing so may result in fines, community service, and other sanctions.
Explanation: In California, it's against the law to give alcohol to a child. Offenders who do so risk fines, community service, and attendance at a mandated alcohol education program, among other sanctions.

4. How does marijuana affect a person's capacity for concentration?
Answer: Because marijuana can make it difficult to concentrate, driving might be challenging for some people.
Explanation: Because marijuana can make it difficult to concentrate, it might increase the chance of accidents while a person is trying to drive.

5. In California, what are the legal repercussions of inhalant-impaired driving?

Answer: Driving while impaired by inhalants is prohibited in California and carries the same penalties as driving while impaired by other drugs or alcohol.
Explanation: Driving while intoxicated by inhalants is prohibited in California and carries the same fines, license suspension, and potential jail time as driving while under the influence of other drugs or alcohol.

6. How does weariness affect a person's capacity for making decisions?
Answer: Being tired might make it harder for someone to make wise decisions and make them more likely to take risks.
Explanation: It's crucial to avoid driving while you're fatigued since fatigue can affect your ability to make decisions, which can result in bad decisions and greater risk-taking behavior.

7. In California, what are the legal repercussions of PCP-impaired driving?
Answer: Driving while under the influence of PCP is prohibited in the state of California and may carry penalties comparable to those for driving while intoxicated by other substances.
Explanation: Driving under the influence of PCP is prohibited in California and carries the same fines, license suspension, and potential jail time as driving under the influence of other narcotics or alcohol.

8. How does alcohol affect a person's ability to coordinate their movements and respond quickly?
Answer: Drinking alcohol can make it challenging to execute jobs that call on rapid reflexes or fine motor skills since it slows down coordination and reaction time.
Explanation: Tasks requiring rapid reflexes or fine motor skills, such as operating a vehicle, can be challenging for people who are inebriated because alcohol can affect their coordination and response time.

9. In California, what are the legal repercussions of lying on a chemical test for drugs or alcohol?
Answer: It's against the law and subject to fines, license suspensions, and other sanctions in California to give false information on a chemical test for drugs or alcohol.
Explanation: It is against the law in California to give false information on a chemical test for alcohol or drugs, and doing so can result in fines, license suspensions, and required DUI education programs, among other sanctions.

10. How can distraction affect a person's capacity to keep a vehicle under control?
Answer: Distraction can make it harder for someone to keep control of a car since it diverts their focus from the road and slows down their reflexes.
Explanation: Distractions when driving should be avoided since they can damage a person's ability to retain control of a vehicle by diverting their attention from the road and slowing down their reaction time.

Vehicle operation and maintenance

1. How frequently should a car's cabin air filter be changed?
Answer: The recommended interval for replacing a car's cabin air filter varies depending on the make and model of the car, but typically ranges from 15,000 to 30,000 miles.
Explanation: A car's cabin air filter is in charge of cleaning the air entering the passenger area, enhancing air quality, and safeguarding the HVAC system. Depending on the make and type of the automobile, the suggested replacement period might vary, although it normally falls between 15,000 and 30,000 kilometers.

2. What function does a car's suspension system serve?
Answer: A car's suspension system's job is to reduce handling and stability issues by absorbing shocks and vibrations from the road.
Explanation: A car's suspension system is made to absorb shocks and vibrations from the road, giving the driver and passengers a smooth and comfortable ride while also enhancing handling and stability.

3. How frequently should a car's coolant be replaced?
Answer: The recommended interval for replacing a car's coolant varies depending on the make and model of the car, but typically ranges from 30,000 to 100,000 miles.
Explanation: A car's coolant controls engine temperature, guards against overheating, and shields the engine from corrosion and deposits. Depending on the make and type of the automobile, the suggested replacement period might vary, although it normally falls between 30,000 and 100,000 kilometers.

4. What does the brake fluid in an automobile do?
Answer: The function of braking fluid in a car is to transmit hydraulic pressure from the brake pedal to the brake calipers or drums, allowing the automobile to slow down and stop.
Explanation: In order for an automobile to slow down and stop, the brake fluid is in charge of transmitting hydraulic pressure from the brake pedal to the braking calipers or drums. Additionally, it aids in lubricating and shielding the parts of the brake system.

5. How frequently should a car's wiper blades be replaced?
Answer: Depending on the make and model of the automobile, the recommended time for replacement wiper blades varies from 6 to 2 months.
Explanation: Wiper blades are a crucial part of a car's windshield wiper system and are in charge of cleaning the windshield of rain, snow, and other debris. Depending on the make and model of the vehicle, the recommended time between

replacements is normally between 6 and 12 months.

6. What does the engine oil in an automobile do?
Answer: The purpose of a car's engine oil is to lubricate the engine's moving parts, reduce friction and wear, and help dissipate heat.
Explanation: An automobile's engine oil is in charge of lubricating the moving components of the engine, lowering friction and wear, and aiding in heat dissipation. Additionally, it aids in cleaning and shielding the engine from impurities and deposits.

7. How frequently should an oil change be performed on a car?
Answer: Depending on the make and model of the automobile, the recommended oil change schedule varies from 5 0 0 0 miles to 10 0 0 0 miles.
Explanation: Changing the oil in an automobile entails emptying the old oil from the engine and replacing it with new oil and a fresh oil filter. Depending on the make and model of the vehicle, the suggested period for completing it varies, but is normally between 5,000 and 10,000 miles.

8. What function does a car's power brake booster serve?
Answer: A car's power brake booster helps the driver apply the brakes, which makes it simpler to stop the car and lessens driver fatigue.
Explanation: A car's power brake booster helps the driver apply the brakes, which makes it simpler to stop the car and lessens driver fatigue. Utilizing hydraulic or vacuum support allows for this.

9. How frequently should ignition coils be changed in a car?
Answer: The suggested period for replacing a car's ignition coils varies based on the make and model of the vehicle, but generally speaking, it falls between 1 and 0 miles, or 5 and 0 miles, respectively.
Explanation: In order to ignite the gasoline in the engine's cylinders, a

high voltage must be supplied by the car's ignition coils. Depending on the make and type of the vehicle, the recommended replacement period normally ranges from 100,000 to 150,000 kilometers.

10. What function does the engine air intake system of a car serve?
The answer is that the function of an automobile's engine air intake system is to provide the engine with clean air in order to ensure optimal combustion and performance.
Explanation: To ensure optimal combustion and performance, a car's engine air intake system is in charge of supplying clean air to the engine. This is accomplished by using an air filter, which clears the air of debris, dust, and other impurities before it enters the engine. The temperature and moisture content of the air entering the engine are also controlled by the air intake system, which can have an impact on combustion and engine performance.

Emergency situations and procedures
1. What should you do if your car's headlights suddenly fail while you're driving?
Answer: If you're traveling and your car's headlights go out abruptly, you should reduce your speed, put on your warning lights, and stop in a safe place to examine them.
Explanation: It might be challenging to see the road ahead if your car's headlights suddenly fail. The chance of an accident can be reduced by slowing down, activating your warning lights, and stopping in a secure area to check the headlights.

2. What should you do if a sandstorm or dust storm hits while you're driving?
Answer: If you're traveling and you come across a dust or sandstorm, you should pull over to a safe place, switch off your car lights, and wait until the storm passes.
Explanation: A sandstorm or dust storm can drastically reduce visibility,

making it challenging to see the road in front of you. The chance of an accident can be reduced by stopping in a secure area, turning off your car's lights, and waiting until the storm has passed.

3. What should you do if an animal crosses your path while you are driving?
Answer: If you are driving and come across an animal on the road, slow down, blast your horn, and attempt to avoid hitting the animal without veering into oncoming traffic or off the road.
Explanation: Hitting an animal on the road might result in damage to your car as well as possible animal injury. The likelihood of a collision can be reduced by slowing down, sounding your horn, and making an effort to avoid hitting the animal without veering into oncoming traffic or off the road.

4. What should you do if you come across a flooded road while driving?
Answer: Since it is challenging to determine the depth of the water and the strength of the river, you should turn around and seek an alternative route if you are driving and come across a flooded road.
Explanation: Driving across a flooded road can be hazardous since it increases the risk of having your car stall out or getting swept away by the current. The possibility of a collision or vehicle damage can be reduced by turning around and choosing an alternative route.

5. What should you do if you come across a downed power line while driving?
Answer: If you are traveling and come across a downed electrical line, you should remain inside your car and phone 911 to report it.
Explanation: Because it may transmit an electrical current, a downed power line can be extremely dangerous. When contacting the car and the ground at the same time, an electrical charge might enter your body, thus

it's crucial to stay inside the car and phone 911 to report the downed power line.

6. What actions should you take if a small collision occurs while you are driving?
Answer: If you are driving and are in a small collision, you should relocate your car to a safe area, swap contact and insurance information with the other motorist, and take pictures and make notes on what happened.
Explanation: To prevent creating further accidents after a small incident, it's crucial to transfer your car to a safe area. To assist with any insurance claims or legal difficulties, exchange contact and insurance information with the other motorist and record the occurrence with photographs and notes.

7. What should you do if you hear a loud banging or knocking sound coming from the engine of your car while you are driving?
Answer: If you are driving and you hear a loud banging or knocking sound coming from your vehicle's engine, you should pull over to a safe location and turn off the engine to avoid causing further damage.
Explanation: A loud banging or knocking noise coming from the engine of your car might be a sign of a significant issue, such a mechanical breakdown or low oil. In order to prevent more damage or the possibility of a breakdown, it is crucial to stop the vehicle in a safe area and turn off the engine.

8. What should you do if you find one of your tires has blown out while you are driving?
Answer: If you are driving and one of your tires blows out, you should hold on to the steering wheel tightly, let off the gas pedal, and guide your car to a safe place to stop.
Explanation: It could be challenging to operate the car if one of your tires blows out. The chance of an accident can be reduced by maintaining a strong grip on the steering wheel,

easing off the gas pedal, and directing the car to a safe spot to stop it.

9. What should you do if a traffic signal is malfunctioning while you're driving?
Answer: If a traffic light fails to function while you are driving, proceed with care and regard the junction as a four-way stop.
Explanation: Determining the right of way might be challenging when a traffic light is not functioning. The chance of an accident can be reduced by moving cautiously and treating the junction as a four-way stop.

10. What should you do if you believe your car's steering is sloppy or sluggish while you're driving?
Answer: If you're behind the wheel of a car and you discover that the steering seems sloppy or sluggish, you should grasp the wheel tightly and drive the car to a secure stop.
Explanation: It may be difficult to operate the car and may indicate a significant issue if the steering is slack or sluggish. To reduce the chance of a collision or vehicle damage, hold the steering wheel firmly and direct the car to a safe place to stop.

Practice Test 8:
Traffic laws, Driving rules and regulations

1. In California, what is the top speed limit for cars on a two-lane divided highway?
Answer: In California, the top speed limit for cars on a two-lane, undivided roadway is 55 mph.
Explanation: The maximum permitted speed for a vehicle to go on a certain road or highway is known as the speed limit. In California, unless otherwise indicated, the top speed limit for cars traveling on a two-lane, undivided roadway is 55 mph.

2. Which lane on a motorway with many lanes should you choose for passing?

Answer: When driving on a multi-lane highway, you should use the left lane for passing.
Explanation: On a highway with many lanes, the left lane is often designated for passing, while the right lane is utilized for slower-moving traffic or for entering or leaving the highway. It's crucial to keep the right lane open at all times and to only utilize the left lane for passing as soon as it's safe to do so.

3. What is California's legal blood alcohol content (BAC) limit for drivers?
Answer: BAC of 0 to 8 percent is the legal limit for drivers in California.
Explanation: In California, it is prohibited to operate a vehicle with a blood alcohol content (BAC) of 0.08% or more. There is a zero-tolerance policy for any level of alcohol in a driver's system under the age of 21.

4. When kids are around, what is the permitted speed in a school zone?
Answer: When there are kids around, the speed restriction in a school zone is 25 mph.
Explanation: When there are kids around, California's school zones have a 25 mph speed restriction. Children who may be crossing the street or walking to or from school need to be protected.

5. What actions should you take in the event of a collision?
Answer: If you are in an accident, you should stop your car right away and exchange contact information with the other driver or drivers.
Explanation: If you are in an accident, you should stop your car right away and exchange contact information with any other drivers who were also there. Your name, address, contact information, insurance details, and car registration information are all included. If there are injuries, major property damage, or if the other driver(s) involved do not have insurance, you should also call the police to report the crash.

6. On a California highway, what is the top speed limit for cars pulling another car?
Answer: On California highways, a car can only go at a maximum speed of 5 mph when pulling another car.
Explanation: Unless otherwise indicated, the top speed restriction on a California roadway is 55 mph when towing another vehicle.

7. What does it indicate when there is a solid yellow line across the road?
The answer is that passing is not permitted when there is a solid yellow line on the road.
Explanation: Passing is prohibited when there is a solid yellow line across the road. When there is a strong yellow line on their side of the road, drivers shouldn't try to pass other cars.

8. What should you do when a railroad crossing has bells blaring and flashing lights?
Answer: You should stop and wait for the train to pass when you approach a railroad crossing with flashing lights and ringing bells.
Explanation: You should stop and wait for the train to pass when you approach a railroad crossing with flashing lights and ringing bells. Never attempt to cross the tracks ahead of a train or get around lowered crossing gates.

9. How far behind the car in front should drivers keep their following distance at all times?
Answer: The minimum following distance that drivers should maintain behind the vehicle in front of them is three seconds.
Explanation: Drivers should keep a safe following distance behind the car in front of them to prevent crashes. The required following distance in California is three seconds, giving drivers adequate time to respond to rapid changes in traffic.

10. What is the top speed allowed through a school zone when classes are in session?

Answer: During school hours, 25 mph is the maximum speed allowed when going through a school zone.
Explanation: The top speed restriction when driving in a school zone during school hours is 25 mph. Children who may be crossing the street or walking to or from school need to be protected.

11. What does it signify when there is a solid white line across the road?
Answer: Lane changes are discouraged if there is a firm white line on the road.
Explanation: A solid white line painted on the road designates a zone where lane changes are not recommended. Drivers should only swerve to avoid traffic and should never cross a solid white line unless it is absolutely essential.

12. What should you do if a tire blowout occurs unexpectedly while you are driving?
Answer: If a tire blows out abruptly while you're driving, you should maintain a tight hold on the wheel and steadily reduce speed.
Explanation: It's crucial to maintain composure and a strong hold on the steering wheel if a tire blows out while you're driving. When it is safe to do so, gradually reduce your speed and pull over to the side of the road. Avoid abrupt maneuvers or slamming on the brakes since they might make the car lose control. Once you have safely stopped, examine the tire and, if required, change it or ask for help.

13. In California, what is the top speed limit on a two-lane highway?
Answer: In California, a two-lane highway's top speed limit is 55 mph.
Explanation: In California, unless otherwise indicated, the top speed limit on a two-lane roadway is 55 mph.

14. What does it signify when there is a solid yellow line on the road next to a broken yellow line?
Answer: Passing is permitted on the side with the broken line but not the

solid line if there is a solid yellow line next to it.
Explanation: When there is a solid yellow line next to a broken yellow line on the road, it means that passing is permitted on the side with the broken line but not on the side with the solid line. Only when it is safe to do so should drivers pass on the side with the broken yellow line.

15. In California, what is the top speed limit on a highway?
Answer: In California, the speed limit is set at 6 5 mph.
Explanation: In California, unless otherwise specified, the top speed limit on a roadway is 65 mph.

16. What should you do when a roundabout approaches?
Answer: Slow down and give way to any oncoming traffic when you approach a roundabout.
Explanation: It's necessary to slow down and surrender to any traffic that is already in a roundabout while approaching one. Enter the roundabout once it is safe to do so, then choose the exit you want by following the guidance signs.

17. In California, what is the top speed limit for driving in a commercial or residential area?
Answer: In California, the top speed restriction for drivers in commercial and residential areas is 25 mph.
Explanation: In California, unless otherwise marked, the top speed restriction when driving in a commercial or residential area is 25 mph.

18. What does it indicate when a red traffic light flashes?
Answer: A flashing red traffic light tells motorists to halt at the intersection.
Explanation: Drivers should stop completely while approaching a flashing red traffic light and only go forward once it is safe to do so. The guidelines for a stop sign are comparable to these.

19. What should you do if a wet road causes your car to hydroplane?
Answer: To restore traction if your car hydroplanes on a wet road, gently depress the gas pedal and keep driving straight.
Explanation: When a car hydroplanes on a wet road, it loses grip and may skid or spin out of control. Regain control by letting up on the throttle and braking gradually. Straighten your steering until you regain traction, then softly press the brake pedal.

20. On a two-lane highway with a 70 mph advertised speed restriction, what is the top speed allowed?
Answer: On a two-lane roadway with a written speed restriction of 0 to 7 mph, the maximum speed limit is 5 to 7 mph.
Explanation: On a two-lane highway with a written speed restriction of 70 mph, the top speed limit is 55 mph. In order to protect both drivers and passengers on the roadway, this is being done.

Road signs and signals
1. What does a red symbol in the shape of an octagon mean?
Answer: A red octagon-shaped sign indicates a stop sign.
Explanation: A stop sign is designated by a red octagon-shaped sign. Even if there is no other traffic present, drivers are still required to stop completely at a stop sign before moving forward.

2. What does a yellow symbol with a diamond shape mean?
Answer: A yellow diamond-shaped sign indicates a warning or caution.
Explanation: A yellow diamond-shaped sign is intended to warn or alert people. This can include alerts for approaching bends, junctions, or other driving dangers.

3. What does an illuminated green circle symbol mean?
Answer: A green circle-shaped sign indicates a permitted action or direction.

Explanation: A green circle-shaped sign is used to indicate a permitted action or direction. This might be moving instructions, such as turn arrows, or parking or loading guidance.

4. What is the meaning of a white rectangle with red lettering?
Answer: A regulatory sign is a white rectangle with red wording.
Explanation: A regulatory sign is identified by a white rectangle-shaped sign with red text. This could contain signs indicating the posted speed limit, no parking zones, or other traffic regulations.

5. What does a circular symbol with a "X" in it, made of yellow and black, mean?
Answer: A yellow and black circular-shaped sign with a "X" indicates a railroad crossing ahead.
Explanation: A railroad crossing is indicated by a circular yellow and black sign with a "X" in it. Drivers ought to reduce their speed and be ready to stop if required.

6. What does a sign with a triangle form in red and white mean?
Answer: A yield sign is identified by a red and white triangle sign.
Explanation: A yield sign is denoted by a red and white triangle symbol. Before moving forward, drivers must yield to pedestrians or other vehicles that have the right-of-way.

7. What does a sign with a blue circle on it mean?
Answer: A blue circle-shaped notice designating a required activity.
Explanation: A sign with a blue circle on it designates a required activity. This might include signs that specify a needed activity, such as one-way or speed restriction signs.

8. What is the meaning of a brown rectangle sign?
Answer: A brown rectangular-shaped sign indicates a recreational or scenic area.

Explanation: A brown rectangular sign used to designate a scenic or recreational area is rectangular in shape. Parks, campsites, and other tourist attractions may fall under this category.

9. What does a rectangle symbol in red and white with diagonal lines mean?
Answer: A do not enter sign is a rectangular red and white sign with diagonal lines.
Explanation: A do not enter sign is identified by a rectangular-shaped sign in red and white with diagonal lines. The route or lane that is indicated by the sign must not be entered by drivers.

10. What does a rectangle sign in yellow and black with an arrow pointing downwards mean?
Answer: A steep hill or downhill is indicated by a rectangular sign in yellow and black with an arrow pointing downward.
Explanation: To signify a severe decline or hill, a rectangular sign in yellow and black with an arrow pointing downhill is utilized. When driving up a steep incline or down a downhill, motorists should slow down and use caution.

11. What does a circular symbol in red and white with a line through it mean?
Answer: A red and white circular-shaped sign with a line through it indicates a no parking zone.
Explanation: A no parking zone is designated by a circular red and white sign with a line through it. Drivers are not permitted to park in the designated area.

12. What does a rectangular sign with a diamond-shaped center that is yellow and black mean?
Answer: A warning of a dangerous item is shown by a rectangular sign with the colors yellow and black and a diamond-shaped emblem in the center.

Explanation: A warning sign for a hazardous item is a rectangular-shaped sign in yellow and black with a diamond-shaped indentation in the center. This might contain warning signs for explosives, flammable substances, or other hazardous substances.

13. What is the meaning of a white rectangular sign with green lettering?
Answer: A white rectangular-shaped sign with green lettering indicates a guide sign.
Explanation: A guiding sign is identified by a white rectangular sign with green text. This might contain highway exit signs, travel times to cities or towns, or other destination details.

14. What does a rectangle symbol in red and white with horizontal lines mean?
Answer: A pedestrian crossing is designated by a rectangular sign in red and white with horizontal lines.
Explanation: To designate a pedestrian crossing, a rectangular-shaped sign in red and white with horizontal lines is utilized. Drivers are required to stop for pedestrians in crosswalks.

15. What does a white wheelchair emblem on a blue rectangular sign mean?
Answer: A parking area designated for people with disabilities is marked with a blue rectangular sign with a white wheelchair emblem.
Explanation: A parking area designated for people with disabilities is marked with a blue rectangular sign with a white wheelchair emblem. These parking spaces provide those who need mobility aids or assistance more room and are frequently found close to building entrances.

16. What does a rectangle sign in green with white letters mean?
Answer: A guidance sign for a particular area or destination is a green rectangular sign with white letters.

Explanation: A guide sign for a particular area or destination is a green rectangular sign with white text. Signs for parks, hospitals, and other tourist attractions may fall under this category.

17. What does a circular sign in yellow and black with a black arrow pointing to the right mean?
Answer: There is a sharp right turn ahead, marked by a circular yellow and black sign with a black arrow pointing in that direction.
Explanation: To signify a steep bend to the right ahead, there is a yellow and black circular sign with a black arrow curving to the right. Drivers should reduce their speed and make sure they are ready to make the turn safely.

18. What is the meaning of a brown circular sign with a white tent symbol?
Answer: A brown circular-shaped sign with a white tent symbol indicates a camping area.
Explanation: A camping area is designated by a brown circular sign with a white tent emblem. Signs for RV parks, campsites, and other camping facilities may fall under this category.

19. What is the meaning of a white rectangular sign with a red circle and a diagonal line?
Answer: A no entrance sign is a white rectangle with a red circle and a diagonal line.
Explanation: A no entrance sign is identified by a white rectangular sign with a red circle and diagonal line. The route or lane that is indicated by the sign must not be entered by drivers.

20. What does a circular symbol in yellow and black with a black arrow pointing upwards mean?
Answer: A steep climb or upgrade is indicated by a circular yellow and black sign with a black arrow pointing uphill.

Explanation: A steep hill or upgrade is identified by a yellow and black circular sign with a black arrow pointing upwards. When driving on a steep incline or upgrade, motorists should reduce their speed and use caution.

Safe driving practices, pedestrians, and bicyclists

1. What should you do if you see a pedestrian crossing the road in a place where there isn't a crosswalk?
Answer: You should yield to the pedestrian and give them the right of way.
Explanation: Whether or not a pedestrian is crossing at a designated crosswalk, they always have the right of way. When a pedestrian crosses the roadway, drivers should yield and allow them plenty of room.

2. When is it OK to turn on your warning lights while driving?
Answer: You should only turn on your hazard lights when your car is immobilized or stopped at the side of the road.
Explanation: Hazard lights are intended to indicate that a vehicle is stopped or disabled on the side of the road. As they may confuse other drivers and cause an accident, they shouldn't be used while driving.

3. When kids are around, what is the permitted speed in a school zone?
Answer: When there are kids around, the speed restriction in a school zone is 25 mph.
Explanation: Designated school zones are places close to schools where it is anticipated that children may be present. The speed restriction is 25 mph when there are kids around to protect their safety.

4. What should be your minimum safe following distance from the car in front of you?
Answer: Three seconds is the recommended minimum safe trailing distance behind the car in front of you.

Explanation: To prevent accidents, it's critical to have a safe following distance. In order to give yourself adequate time to respond in the event that the car in front of you suddenly stops or slows down, you should maintain a following distance of at least three seconds.

5. What should you do if a bike is using the center of the road?
Answer: You should reduce your speed and wait until it is safe to overtake the bicycle, giving them at least three feet of space.
Explanation: If they believe it is important for their safety, bicycles are permitted to ride in the centre of a lane. When passing, drivers should slow down and allow them plenty of room.

6. When is using a cell phone while driving in California permitted?
Answer: Only when utilizing a hands-free device is it acceptable to use a cell phone while operating a motor vehicle in California.
Explanation: California law prohibits drivers from holding a cell phone while driving. Only while utilizing a hands-free gadget like a Bluetooth headset or loudspeaker is there an exemption.

7. What should you do if another vehicle also stops at a four-way intersection?
Answer: The vehicle on the right has the right of way. If two cars arrive simultaneously, the one on the right should move forward first.
Explanation: At a four-way stop, cars are required to yield to one another in a particular sequence. If two cars arrive simultaneously, the one on the right should move forward first.

8. When should you drive while using your high beams?
Answer: When traveling in rural regions without any other cars or lighting, you should use your high beams.
Explanation: When driving in places without other cars or lamps, high

beams are used to increase visibility. When driving in cities or when you are close to other cars, you should turn them off.

9. What should you do if you observe a blind person crossing the road with a white cane or a guide dog?
Answer: You should halt your progress and wait until the pedestrian has successfully crossed the roadway.
Explanation: Guide dogs or white canes are used by blind people to cross the roadway. Before moving forward, drivers should stop and wait for a pedestrian to cross the street safely.

10. What should you do if you are driving and you see a roundabout?
Answer: Go more slowly and give way to any oncoming traffic on the roundabout.
Explanation: Traffic moves counterclockwise around roundabouts, which are circular crossings. Before entering the roundabout, motorists should slow down and yield to oncoming traffic.

Alcohol and drug awareness
1. What is the legal blood alcohol concentration (BAC) limit for drivers over 21 years old in California?
Answer: In California, 0.08% is the legal blood alcohol content limit for drivers older than 21.
Explanation: It is forbidden to drive in California with a blood alcohol content (BAC) of 0.08% or higher. For commercial drivers and drivers under the age of 21, this restriction is lower.

2. What is the legislation governing implied consent?
Answer: According to the implied consent rule, drivers who are suspected of DUI must submit to a chemical test if requested by a law enforcement official.
Explanation: If a law enforcement official requests it, drivers in California who are suspected of driving under the influence must take a chemical test. The suspension of a driver's license might happen if you refuse to take the exam.

3. In California, what is the punishment for a first-time DUI conviction?
Answer: In California, a first-time DUI conviction carries a range of penalties, including fines, license suspension, probation, and jail time.
Explanation: The penalties for a DUI conviction in California can be severe, even for a first-time offender. A first-time offender may also be compelled to take alcohol education programs, serve probation, or go to jail in addition to paying penalties and having their license suspended.

4. What does California's "per se" statute entail?
Answer: Under California's "per se" statute, a driver may be charged with DUI regardless of whether they are genuinely impaired by alcohol or other drugs.
Explanation: Under California's "per se" rule, a driver may be prosecuted with DUI even though they do not appear to be intoxicated if their blood alcohol content is over the legal limit. This is so that there is no doubt that you are impaired if your BAC is beyond the legal limit.

5. In California, what is the consequence for denying a chemical test when charged with DUI?
Answer: In California, a driver's license suspension and fines may result from rejecting a chemical test when they are suspected of driving under the influence.
Explanation: In California, drivers who refuse to take a chemical test when they are suspected of driving under the influence may be subject to fines and license suspension.

6. What does a field sobriety test involve?
Answer: A field sobriety test is a series of physical and cognitive tests used by law enforcement officers to determine if a driver is impaired.

Explanation: Tasks like standing on one leg or walking straight are frequently included in field sobriety tests. Law enforcement officials utilize these tests to gauge a driver's level of intoxication.

7. In California, what is the consequence of a second DUI conviction?
Answer: In California, a second DUI conviction carries a sentence that may include fines, a suspended license, probation, and perhaps jail time.
Explanation: In California, the consequences for a second DUI conviction are more severe than those for a first-time offender. A second offense may result in probation, jail time, alcohol education programs, fines, and license suspension in addition to other penalties.

8. In California, what is the legal blood alcohol limit for business drivers?
Answer: In California, 0.04% is the legal blood alcohol content limit for commercial drivers.
Explanation: In California, the BAC limit for commercial drivers is lower than that for regular drivers. A commercial driver cannot operate a vehicle with a blood alcohol content (BAC) of 0.04% or higher.

9. In California, what is the punishment for a third DUI conviction?
Answer: In California, a third DUI conviction can result in penalties, license suspension, probation, and even jail time.
Explanation: In California, the consequences for a third DUI conviction are much harsher than those for a first offense. A third offense may result in probation, jail time, alcohol education programs, fines, and license revocation in addition to other penalties.

10. What distinguishes a DUI from a DWI?

Answer: DWI stands for driving while drunk; DUI stands for driving while under the influence. Both phrases pertain to operating a vehicle while under the influence of drugs or alcohol in California and are interchangeable.
Explanation: Although the phrases DUI and DWI are occasionally used synonymously, they may have different legal connotations in other states. Both phrases are used to describe driving while under the influence of drugs or alcohol in California.

Vehicle operation and maintenance
1. What should you do if your car overheats while you're driving?
Answer: If your car overheats while you're driving, stop the car in a safe place, then switch off the engine.
Explanation: Your car may sustain significant harm from an overheated engine. If you see that your engine is overheating, stop as soon as you can in a secure area and switch off the engine. Before trying to drive again, let the engine cool down.

2. Why does your dashboard's oil pressure warning light come on?
Answer: Your engine's low oil pressure may be harming it, as indicated by the oil pressure warning light.
Explanation: The oil pressure warning light is a critical sign of the condition of your engine. If the indicator illuminates while you're driving, your engine's oil pressure is likely low and might be resulting in harm. As soon as possible, you should stop driving and check your oil level.

3. How frequently should you change the oil in your engine?
Answer: The recommended interval for changing your engine oil varies depending on the make and model of your vehicle, but is typically around every 5,000 to 7,500 miles.
Explanation: Changing your engine oil on a regular basis is essential for keeping your car in good condition.

Depending on the make and model of your car, the recommended time between oil changes varies, but is normally between 5,000 and 7,500 miles.

4. What should you do if the brakes on your car fail while you're driving?
Answer: If your car's brakes fail while you're driving, you should pump the brakes and downshift to a lower gear to slow down.
Explanation: Having a car's brakes fail while you're driving might be scary. Nevertheless, there are steps you may take to slow down and stop your car. Start by pumping the brakes to create pressure. After then, downshift to a lower gear to slow the car down. Finally, stop the car by using the emergency brake.

5. What function does your car's tire pressure monitoring system (TPMS) serve?
Answer: The TPMS is built to notify you when one or more of your tires have low tire pressure.
Explanation: The TPMS is an important safety feature in modern vehicles. It is made to notify you when one or more of your tires have low tire pressure, which can assist avoid accidents and increase fuel efficiency.

6. How frequently should you change the air filter in your car?
Answer: The recommended interval for replacing your vehicle's air filter varies depending on the make and model of your vehicle, but is typically around every 12,000 to 15,000 miles.
Explanation: The air filter is a crucial part of the engine of your car because it prevents dirt and debris from entering the engine. Depending on the make and model of your car, the recommended time between air filter changes is generally between 12,000 and 15,000 miles.

7. What should you do if the battery in your car fails while you're driving?

Answer: If your car battery fails while you're driving, pull over safely to the side of the road and dial 911.
Explanation: It may be challenging to keep driving if your car's battery fails in the middle of a trip. To safely restart the battery while driving, safely pull over to the side of the road and make a call for help.

8. What does the coolant in the engine of your car do?
Answer: By controlling its temperature, the coolant is made to prevent your car's engine from overheating.
Explanation: Your car's engine's coolant is a crucial part since it helps control the engine's temperature and avoid overheating. Regularly checking your coolant level and topping it out as necessary are crucial.

9. How frequently should you replace the brake pads on your car?
Answer: The recommended interval for replacing your vehicle's brake pads varies depending on the make and model of your vehicle, but is typically around every 50,000 miles.
Explanation: Brake pads are a crucial part of your car's braking system since they aid in slowing and stopping the car. Depending on the make and model of your car, the suggested time between brake pad replacements varies, but it's normally every 50,000 miles or so.

10. What should you do if steering your car gets challenging while you're driving?
Answer: You should safely pull over to the side of the road and check the amount of your power steering fluid if steering in your car gets challenging while you're driving.
Explanation: Steering difficulty may indicate a problem with your car's power steering system. Check the amount of your power steering fluid and carefully pull over to the side of the road if you discover that steering has gotten challenging. If there is a low fluid level, top it off and keep

going. Contact a mechanic for assistance if the issue continues.

Emergency situations and procedures

1. In the event of an automobile accident, what should you do first?
Answer: After an automobile collision, you should check on everyone's safety and dial 911 if required.
Explanation: After an automobile collision, safety should come first. In case of an emergency, check to see if anyone is hurt and dial 911. Share information with the other motorist or drivers and, if at all feasible, take pictures of the collision.

2. What actions should you take if a power line comes down while you're driving?
Answer: You should stay in your car and dial 911 if you come across a downed power line while driving.
Explanation: Fallen power wires may be quite hazardous. If you come over a downed power line while driving, don't try to get out. Keep inside and dial 911 instead. Inform others to avoid the area.

3. What actions should you take if your car breaks down on a busy road?
Answer: If you can, relocate your car to the shoulder of a major highway if it breaks down, and switch on your hazard lights.
Explanation: If your car breaks down on a major highway, you should relocate it to the shoulder as quickly as you can to prevent creating a safety problem for other drivers. To alert other vehicles, turn on your warning lights.

4. When driving, how much space should be maintained between your car and the one in front of you?
Answer: When driving, it's advised to allow at least two seconds between your car and the one in front of you.
Explanation: Maintaining a safe following distance is crucial for avoiding accidents. It is advised to allow at least two seconds between your car and the one in front of you. In bad weather, extend this distance further.

5. What should you do if a wildfire catches your attention as you're travelling in California?
Answer: In the event that you come across a wildfire while traveling in California, you should heed the instructions of emergency services and, if necessary, flee the area.
Explanation: Wildfires may be incredibly unpredictable and hazardous. Follow the instructions of emergency services if you come across a wildfire while traveling in California and leave the area if necessary.

6. What actions should you take if your brakes fail while you're driving?
Answer: If your brakes fail while you're driving, downshift into a lower gear and slow down using the emergency brake.
Explanation: Having your brakes fail while you're driving might be unnerving. Nevertheless, there are steps you may take to slow down and stop your car. To start slowing down the car, downshift to a lower gear. After then, stop the car by using the emergency brake.

7. What should you do if you are traveling and come across a flash flood?
Answer: If a flash flood occurs while you are driving, you should reverse and locate an alternative path.
Explanation: Vehicles can be suddenly overwhelmed by flash floods, which are quite dangerous. Turn back and find an alternative route if you are driving and come across a flash flood. Never try to drive across an area that is flooded.

8. What should you do if it's foggy outside and you're driving?
Answer: You should slow down and utilize your low-beam headlights if you are driving in foggy circumstances.

Explanation: Driving vision can be significantly reduced by fog. In order to increase visibility while driving in foggy weather, slow down and turn on your low-beam headlights. Use low beams alone; high beams can reflect off the fog and make it much more difficult to see.

9. What should you do if you see someone hit and run?
Answer: If you witness a hit-and-run accident, you should try to get the license plate number of the fleeing vehicle and call 911.
Explanation: Hit-and-run incidents may be dangerous and irritating. If you see a hit-and-run collision, attempt to record the license plate number of the evading car and report the event to the police by dialing 911.

10. What should you do if a tornado crosses your path while you're driving?
Answer: If a tornado strikes while you are driving, you should stop and take cover in a strong structure, or if that is not an option, lay flat in a ditch or other low-lying location.
Explanation: Tornadoes have the potential to be quite destructive and seriously harm cars. If a tornado strikes while you're driving, try to find cover within a strong structure. If it's not practicable, lay down and cover your head with your hands in a ditch or other low-lying place.

Bonus Chapter 1: 120 California DMV Exam Most Frequently Asked Questions

1. When should you use your turn signals?
A) Only when changing lanes
B) Only when turning
C) When changing lanes or turning
D) None of the above

2. What is the maximum speed limit in a residential area?
A) 15 mph
B) 25 mph
C) 35 mph
D) 45 mph

3. When is it legal to use a cell phone while driving in California?
A) When using a hands-free device
B) When making an emergency call
C) When parked on the side of the road
D) None of the above

4. What is the penalty for driving under the influence (DUI) in California?
A) A fine of up to $1,000
B) License suspension for up to 6 months
C) Jail time and license suspension
D) All of the above

5. What should you do if you are involved in a collision?
A) Stop immediately and exchange information
B) Keep driving to avoid traffic congestion
C) Call the police to report the collision
D) None of the above

6. What is the minimum age to obtain a driver's license in California?
A) 16 years old
B) 17 years old
C) 18 years old
D) 21 years old

7. When is it legal to make a U-turn?

A) Whenever there is no sign prohibiting it
B) Only at intersections with a traffic light
C) Only on one-way streets
D) None of the above

8. What is the penalty for driving with a suspended or revoked license in California?
A) A fine of up to $1,000
B) Jail time and a longer license suspension
C) Both A and B
D) None of the above

9. When should you use your high beams?
A) In foggy weather
B) In heavy traffic
C) When driving on a well-lit street
D) None of the above

10. What is the maximum speed limit on California highways?
A) 55 mph
B) 65 mph
C) 70 mph
D) 75 mph

11. What is the penalty for speeding in a construction zone in California?
A) A fine of up to $1,000
B) License suspension for up to 6 months
C) Both A and B
D) None of the above

12. What is the penalty for driving without insurance in California?
A) A fine of up to $500
B) License suspension and impounding of the vehicle
C) Both A and B
D) None of the above

13. When should you yield to pedestrians?
A) Only in marked crosswalks

B) Only when the pedestrian is in the crosswalk
C) Whenever a pedestrian is crossing the street
D) None of the above

14. What is the penalty for driving without a valid driver's license in California?
A) A fine of up to $1,000
B) Jail time and impounding of the vehicle
C) Both A and B
D) None of the above

15. When is it legal to pass another vehicle on the right?
A) Only on one-way streets
B) Only on highways with two or more lanes in each direction
C) Only in heavy traffic
D) None of the above

16. What should you do if you miss your exit on the freeway?
A) Back up and exit at the next off-ramp
B) Continue driving and exit at the next off-ramp
C) Stop on the freeway and wait for assistance
D) None of the above

17. What is the penalty for driving with an expired registration in California?
A) A fine of up to $500
B) License suspension and impounding of the vehicle
C) Both A and B
D) None of the above

18. When is it legal to park in a bike lane?
A) Never
B) Only when there is no other parking available
C) Only for a short period of time to drop off or pick up passengers
D) None of the above

19. What is the penalty for passing a stopped school bus with its red lights flashing?
A) A fine of up to $1,000

B) License suspension for up to 6 months
C) Both A and B
D) None of the above

20. When is it legal to make a left turn on a red light?
A) Only when turning onto a one-way streetB) Only when turning onto a two-way street
C) Only when there is no sign prohibiting it
D) Never

21. What is the penalty for reckless driving in California?
A) A fine of up to $1,000
B) Jail time and license suspension
C) Both A and B
D) None of the above

22. What is the minimum following distance you should maintain behind the vehicle in front of you?
A) 1 second
B) 2 seconds
C) 3 seconds
D) 4 seconds

23. When should you use your hazard lights?
A) When driving in heavy rain
B) When driving in heavy traffic
C) When stopped on the side of the road
D) None of the above

24. What is the penalty for driving a vehicle that emits excessive smoke or fumes?
A) A fine of up to $500
B) License suspension and impounding of the vehicle
C) Both A and B
D) None of the above

25. When should you use your horn?
A) To warn other drivers of your presence
B) To express frustration or anger
C) To greet someone you know
D) None of the above

26. What is the penalty for driving with a blood alcohol content (BAC) of 0.08% or higher in California?

A) A fine of up to $1,000
B) Jail time and license suspension
C) Both A and B
D) None of the above

27. When is it legal to pass another vehicle on the left?
A) Only on highways with two or more lanes in each direction
B) Only when the vehicle in front of you is turning left
C) Only when there is no oncoming traffic
D) None of the above

28. What is the penalty for driving with an open container of alcohol in California?
A) A fine of up to $250
B) Jail time and license suspension
C) Both A and B
D) None of the above

29. When is it legal to drive in a bike lane?
A) Only when turning right at an intersection
B) Never
C) Only to pass a slower-moving vehicle
D) None of the above

30. What is the penalty for driving without a seat belt in California?
A) A fine of up to $200
B) License suspension and impounding of the vehicle
C) Both A and B
D) None of the above

31. When should you use your headlights?
A) Only at night or in low visibility conditions
B) Only when driving on a highway
C) Only when driving in heavy traffic
D) None of the above

32. What is the penalty for driving too slowly on the freeway in California?
A) A fine of up to $200
B) License suspension and impounding of the vehicle
C) Both A and B
D) None of the above

33. When is it legal to pass another vehicle on the right shoulder?
A) Only in heavy traffic
B) Only when the vehicle in front of you is turning left
C) Never
D) None of the above

34. What is the penalty for driving with a suspended or revoked registration in California?
A) A fine of up to $500
B) License suspension and impounding of the vehicle
C) Both A and B
D) None of the above

35. When is it legal to make a right turn on a red light?
A) Only when turning onto a one-way street
B) Only when turning onto a two-way street
C) Only when there is no sign prohibiting it
D) Never

36. What is the penalty for leaving the scene of a collision in California?
A) A fine of up to $1,000
B) Jail time and license suspension
C) Both A and B
D) None of the above

37. When is it legal to use studded tires in California?
A) Only during the winter months
B) Only if you live in a mountainous area
C) Never
D) None of the above

38. What is the penalty for driving too closely to the vehicle in front of you in California?
A) A fine of up to $250
B) License suspension and impounding of the vehicle
C) Both A and B
D) None of the above

39. When should you use your emergency flashers?
A) When driving in a funeral procession
B) When driving in a parade

C) When your vehicle is disabled on the side of the road
D) None of the above

40. What is the penalty for driving a vehicle with tires worn down to the wear bars?
A) A fine of up to $500
B) License suspension and impounding of the vehicle
C) Both A and B
D) None of the above

41. What is the penalty for driving a vehicle with excessively tinted windows?
A) A fine of up to $250
B) License suspension and impounding of the vehicle
C) Both A and B
D) None of the above

42. When is it legal to drive in a carpool lane?
A) Only with two or more passengers in the vehicle
B) Only during rush hour
C) Only with a special permit
D) None of the above

43. What is the penalty for driving with a suspended or revoked driver's license in California?
A) A fine of up to $1,000
B) Jail time and license suspension
C) Both A and B
D) None of the above

44. When should you use your windshield wipers?
A) Only in heavy rain
B) Only in light rain
C) Only when driving on the freeway
D) None of the above

45. What is the maximum speed limit in a school zone when children are present?
A) 15 mph
B) 20 mph
C) 25 mph
D) 30 mph

46. When is it legal to drive on the shoulder of the road?
A) Only in an emergency

B) Only to pass a slower-moving vehicle
C) Never
D) None of the above

47. What is the penalty for driving without a valid registration in California?
A) A fine of up to $500
B) License suspension and impounding of the vehicle
C) Both A and B
D) None of the above

48. When should you use your fog lights?
A) Only in heavy fog
B) Only in light fog
C) Only when driving on the freeway
D) None of the above

49. What is the penalty for driving a vehicle with expired tags in California?
A) A fine of up to $500
B) License suspension and impounding of the vehicle
C) Both A and B
D) None of the above

50. When is it legal to park in a handicap parking space?
A) Only with a valid handicap parking permit
B) Only when no other parking spaces are available
C) Only for a short period of time to drop off or pick up someone with a disability
D) None of the above

51. What is the penalty for driving in a bike lane in California?
A) A fine of up to $250
B) License suspension and impounding of the vehicle
C) Both A and B
D) None of the above

52. When is it legal to make a U-turn at a traffic light?
A) Only when there is a green arrow indicating a U-turn is allowed
B) Only when there is no sign prohibiting a U-turn
C) Never

D) None of the above

53. What is the penalty for driving with an expired driver's license in California?
A) A fine of up to $250
B) License suspension and impounding of the vehicle
C) Both A and B
D) None of the above

54. When should you use your parking brake?
A) Only when parked on a hill
B) Only when parked on a flat surface
C) Only when driving on a steep grade
D) None of the above

55. What is the penalty for driving a vehicle with a loud exhaust system in California?
A) A fine of up to $250
B) License suspension and impounding of the vehicle
C) Both A and B
D) None of the above

56. When is it legal to use your cell phone while driving in California?
A) Only when using a hands-free device
B) Only when making an emergency call
C) Only when stopped on the side of the road
D) None of the above

57. What is the penalty for driving a vehicle with a broken tail light in California?
A) A fine of up to $250
B) License suspension and impounding of the vehicle
C) Both A and B
D) None of the above

58. When should you use your headlights on high beam?
A) Only in heavy fog
B) Only on poorly lit roads
C) Only when driving in heavy traffic
D) None of the above

59. What is the penalty for driving without a valid insurance policy in California?
A) A fine of up to $500
B) License suspension and impounding of the vehicle
C) Both A and B
D) None of the above

60. When is it legal to pass another vehicle on the left shoulder?
A) Only in heavy traffic
B) Only when the vehicle in front of you is turning left
C) Never
D) None of the above

61. What is the penalty for driving a vehicle with a cracked windshield in California?
A) A fine of up to $250
B) License suspension and impounding of the vehicle
C) Both A and B
D) None of the above

62. When should you use your hazard lights?
A) Only when parked on the side of the road
B) Only when driving in heavy rain or fog
C) Only when there is an emergency
D) None of the above

63. What is the penalty for driving a vehicle with bald tires in California?
A) A fine of up to $250
B) License suspension and impounding of the vehicle
C) Both A and B
D) None of the above

64. When is it legal to turn right on a red light?
A) Only after coming to a complete stop and yielding to pedestrians and other vehicles
B) Only when there is no sign prohibiting a right turn on red
C) Never
D) None of the above

65. What is the penalty for driving a vehicle with a broken side mirror in California?

A) A fine of up to $250
B) License suspension and impounding of the vehicle
C) Both A and B
D) None of the above

66. When should you use your turn signal?
A) Only when turning left or right
B) Only when changing lanes
C) Only when merging onto a freeway
D) All of the above

67. What is the penalty for driving a vehicle with a missing license plate in California?
A) A fine of up to $250
B) License suspension and impounding of the vehicle
C) Both A and B
D) None of the above

68. When is it legal to pass another vehicle on the right?
A) Only on a one-way street
B) Only when the vehicle in front of you is turning left
C) Only when there are two or more lanes of traffic going in your direction
D) None of the above

69. What is the penalty for driving under the influence (DUI) of drugs or alcohol in California?
A) A fine of up to $10,000
B) Jail time and license suspension
C) Both A and B
D) None of the above

70. When should you use your headlights on low beam?
A) Only in heavy fog
B) Only on poorly lit roads
C) Only when driving in heavy traffic
D) All of the above

71. What is the penalty for driving with an open container of alcohol in California?
A) A fine of up to $1,000
B) License suspension and impounding of the vehicle
C) Both A and B
D) None of the above

72. When is it legal to drive in a bike lane in California?
A) Only when turning left at an intersection
B) Only when there are no bicyclists present
C) Never
D) None of the above

73. What is the penalty for driving a vehicle with a broken headlight in California?
A) A fine of up to $250
B) License suspension and impounding of the vehicle
C) Both A and B
D) None of the above

74. When should you use your horn?
A) Only when there is an emergency
B) Only to warn other drivers of your presence
C) Only when passing another vehicle
D) None of the above

75. What is the penalty for driving a vehicle with a broken brake light in California?
A) A fine of up to $250
B) License suspension and impounding of the vehicle
C) Both A and B
D) None of the above

76. When is it legal to pass another vehicle on a two-lane road?
A) Only when there is a broken yellow line on your side of the road
B) Only when there is a passing lane on your side of the road
C) Only when there is a solid white line on the other side of the road
D) None of the above

77. What is the penalty for driving a vehicle with a missing rearview mirror in California?
A) A fine of up to $250
B) License suspension and impounding of the vehicle
C) Both A and B
D) None of the above

78. When should you yield to pedestrians?

A) Only when they are crossing at a crosswalk
B) Only when they are crossing against a red light
C) Always
D) None of the above

79. What is the penalty for driving a vehicle with a missing seatbelt in California?
A) A fine of up to $250
B) License suspension and impounding of the vehicle
C) Both A and B
D) None of the above

80. When is it legal to drive with your hazard lights on?
A) Only when driving in heavy rain or fog
B) Only when driving on the freeway
C) Only when there is an emergency
D) None

81. What is the penalty for driving a vehicle with excessively worn brakes in California?
A) A fine of up to $250
B) License suspension and impounding of the vehicle
C) Both A and B
D) None of the above

82. When should you use your turn signal when changing lanes?
A) Only after you have completed the lane change
B) Only before you start the lane change
C) Both A and B
D) None of the above

83. What is the penalty for driving a vehicle with a missing taillight in California?
A) A fine of up to $250
B) License suspension and impounding of the vehicle
C) Both A and B
D) None of the above

84. When is it legal to drive on the left side of the road?
A) Only when passing another vehicle
B) Only when turning left at an intersection

C) Only when driving on a one-way street
D) None of the above

85. What is the penalty for driving a vehicle with a broken muffler in California?
A) A fine of up to $250
B) License suspension and impounding of the vehicle
C) Both A and B
D) None of the above

86. When should you use your hazard lights when driving on the freeway?
A) Only when driving in heavy rain or fog
B) Only when you are driving slower than the flow of traffic
C) Only when there is an emergency
D) None of the above

87. What is the penalty for driving a vehicle with a missing side mirror in California?
A) A fine of up to $250
B) License suspension and impounding of the vehicle
C) Both A and B
D) None of the above

88. When should you use your headlights on high beam when driving on the freeway?
A) Only when driving in heavy rain or fog
B) Only when there is no other traffic on the road
C) Only when passing another vehicle
D) None of the above

89. What is the penalty for driving a vehicle with a missing front license plate in California?
A) A fine of up to $250
B) License suspension and impounding of the vehicle
C) Both A and B
D) None of the above

90. When is it legal to park in front of a fire hydrant?
A) Only when there is no other parking available nearby
B) Only for a short period of time to quickly drop off or pick up someone or something

C) Never
D) None of the above

91. What is the penalty for driving a vehicle with a missing turn signal in California?
A) A fine of up to $250
B) License suspension and impounding of the vehicle
C) Both A and B
D) None of the above

92. When is it legal to drive on the shoulder of the road to pass another vehicle?
A) Only in an emergency
B) Only when the other vehicle is turning left
C) Never
D) None of the above

93. What is the penalty for driving a vehicle with a missing brake light in California?
A) A fine of up to $250
B) License suspension and impounding of the vehicle
C) Both A and B
D) None of the above

94. When should you use your emergency flashers?
A) Only when there is an emergency
B) Only when driving slower than the flow of traffic on the freeway
C) Only when driving in heavy rain or fog
D) None of the above

95. What is the penalty for driving a vehicle with a missing rear license plate in California?
A) A fine of up to $250
B) License suspension and impounding of the vehicle
C) Both A and B
D) None of the above

96. When is it legal to make a left turn at a red light?
A) Only when turning from a one-way street onto another one-way street
B) Only when turning from a two-way street onto a one-way street
C) Only when there is no sign prohibiting a left turn on red
D) None of the above

97. What is the penalty for driving a vehicle with a missing headlight in California?
A) A fine of up to $250
B) License suspension and impounding of the vehicle
C) Both A and B
D) None of the above

98. When should you use your headlights on low beam when driving on the freeway?
A) Only when driving in heavy rain or fog
B) Only when there is other traffic on the road
C) Only when passing another vehicle
D) None of the above

99. What is the penalty for driving a vehicle with a missing side window in California?
A) A fine of up to $250
B)License suspension and impounding of the vehicle
C) Both A and B
D) None of the above

100. When is it legal to pass another vehicle on the right side?
A) Only when the other vehicle is turning left and there is an available lane to pass on the right
B) Only when driving on a one-way street with two or more lanes
C) Only when there is an available lane to pass on the right and the road ahead is clear
D) None of the above.

101. When should you use your high beams when driving?
A) When driving in foggy conditions
B) When driving in well-lit urban areas
C) When driving on unlit highways and rural roads
D) None of the above

102. What is the penalty for driving a vehicle with a cracked windshield in California?
A) A fine of up to $250
B) License suspension and impounding of the vehicle

C) Both A and B
D) None of the above

103. When should you use your low beams when driving?
A) When driving in foggy conditions
B) When driving on a well-lit urban street
C) When driving on unlit highways and rural roads
D) None of the above

104. What is the penalty for driving a vehicle with excessively tinted windows in California?
A) A fine of up to $250
B) License suspension and impounding of the vehicle
C) Both A and B
D) None of the above

105. When should you use your headlights when driving in the rain?
A) Only when driving at night
B) Only when driving during the day
C) When driving in rain, fog, snow, or other low-visibility conditions
D) None of the above

106. What is the maximum speed limit on California highways unless otherwise posted?
A) 55 miles per hour
B) 65 miles per hour
C) 70 miles per hour
D) 75 miles per hour

107. What is the maximum speed limit in school zones in California?
A) 15 miles per hour
B) 20 miles per hour
C) 25 miles per hour
D) 30 miles per hour

108. What is the maximum speed limit in residential areas in California?
A) 15 miles per hour
B) 25 miles per hour
C) 35 miles per hour
D) 45 miles per hour

109. What is the penalty for driving under the influence of drugs in California?
A) A fine of up to $1,000

B) License suspension and impounding of the vehicle
C) Both A and B
D) None of the above

110. What is the penalty for driving under the influence of alcohol in California?
A) A fine of up to $1,000
B) License suspension and impounding of the vehicle
C) Both A and B
D) None of the above

111. What is the maximum speed limit for commercial vehicles on California highways?
A) 55 miles per hour
B) 60 miles per hour
C) 65 miles per hour
D) 70 miles per hour

112. What is the penalty for driving without a valid driver's license in California?
A) A fine of up to $250
B) License suspension and impounding of the vehicle
C) Both A and B
D) None of the above

113. In California, what is the minimum age for a person to be eligible for a learner's permit?
A) 14 and a half years
B) 15 years
C) 15 and a half years
D) 16 years

114. What is the penalty for driving without insurance in California?
A) A fine of up to $500
B) License suspension and impounding of the vehicle
C) Both A and B
D) None of the above

115. What is the penalty for littering from a vehicle in California?
A) A fine of up to $1,000
B) License suspension and impounding of the vehicle
C) Both A and B
D) None of the above

116. In California, what is the minimum age for a person to be eligible for a driver's license?
A) 16 years
B) 17 years
C) 18 years
D) 21 years

117. What is the penalty for disobeying a traffic signal in California?
A) A fine of up to $500
B) License suspension and impounding of the vehicle
C) Both A and B
D) None of the above

118. What is the penalty for reckless driving in California?
A) A fine of up to $1,000

B) License suspension and impounding of the vehicle
C) Both A and B
D) None of the above

119. In California, what is the minimum amount of liability insurance that a driver must carry?
A) $10,000
B) $15,000
C) $25,000
D) $30,000

120. What is the penalty for leaving the scene of an accident in California?
A) A fine of up to $1,000
B) License suspension and impounding of the vehicle
C) Both A and B
D) None of the above

Correct answers:

1. C
2. B
3. A
4. C
5. A
6. A
7. A
8. C
9. D
10. C
11. C
12. C
13. C
14. C
15. B
16. B
17. C
18. A
19. C
20. D
21. C

22. C
23. A
24. C
25. A
26. C
27. A
28. A
29. B
30. A
31. A
32. D
33. C
34. A
35. C
36. C
37. C
38. A
39. C
40. A
41. A
42. A

43. C
44. A
45. A
46. A
47. C
48. A
49. A
50. A
51. A
52. B
53. C
54. A
55. A
56. A
57. A
58. B
59. C
60. C
61. A
62. B
63. A

64. A	80. D	96. A
65. A	81. A	97. A
66. D	82. B	98. D
67. A	83. A	99. A
68. C	84. A	100. C
69. B	85. A	101. C
70. D	86. D	102. A
71. A	87. A	103. C
72. C	88. D	104. A
73. A	89. A	105. C
74. B	90. C	106. C
75. A	91. A	107. B
76. A	92. A	108. B
77. A	93. A	109. C
78. C	94. D	110. C
79. A	95. A	111. A
112. C	115. A	118. C
113. B	116. A	
114. C	117. A	
119. C	120. C	

Bonus Chapter 2: Your Link To The Official California DMV Manual

Made in the USA
Las Vegas, NV
09 November 2023